Change Me
Prayers

ALSO BY TOSHA SILVER

Outrageous Openness: Letting the Divine Take the Lead

Make Me Your Own (forthcoming)

Change Me Prayers

THE HIDDEN POWER OF SPIRITUAL SURRENDER

TOSHA SILVER

Foreword by Lissa Rankin, M.D.

ATRIA BOOKS

NEW YORK LONDON TORONTO SYDNEY NEW DELHI

ATRIA BOOKS
A Division of Simon & Schuster, Inc.
1230 Avenue of the Americas
New York, NY 10020

First Atria Books hardcover edition May 2015

ATRIA BOOKS and colophon are trademarks of
Simon & Schuster, Inc.

For information about special discounts for bulk purchases, please
contact Simon & Schuster Special Sales at 1-866-506-1949
or business@simonandschuster.com.

The Simon & Schuster Speakers Bureau can bring authors to your
live event. For more information or to book an event, contact the
Simon & Schuster Speakers Bureau at 1-866-248-3049
or visit our website at www.simonspeakers.com.

Interior design by Paul Dippolito

Manufactured in the United States of America

10   9   8   7   6

Library of Congress Cataloging-in-Publication Data is available.

ISBN 978-1-4767-8976-7
ISBN 978-1-4767-8977-4 (ebook)

*Dedicated to the memory of my beautiful
mother and father, Debbie and Abe Silver*

CONTENTS

CHANGE ME PRAYERS QUICK GUIDE

I found God in Myself and I loved Her, and I loved Her, and I loved Her . . . fiercely.

—NTOZAKE SHANGE

FOREWORD

Ever since I read Tosha's first book, *Outrageous Openness*, I've tried to make my life a devotional act of offering my whole being to the Divine Beloved. This is something I work on daily. At least a dozen times a day, I catch myself trying to control what happens in my life. I can tell I'm evolving, though, because it takes only moments to remember that something Larger can orchestrate life's symphony much more artfully than my ego ever could. The practices Tosha shares have radically changed my existence. Previously, I was chasing what I thought was the holy grail, only to realize it's inside my own heart.

Let me show you how this has worked in my own life in a profound and personal way:

How I dealt with my divorce is just one of many miracles I've experienced since choosing to live from a place of deep surrender. If you make the same choice, you too will experience the trust that it's not only safe to live this way, it's actually where your ultimate safety lies.

After twelve years together, my husband and I made the difficult decision to divorce. For a while, we stayed in the same house to co-parent our daughter. But the time came when we had to face the uncomfortable realities of separating. Despite my highest best intentions, I witnessed my ego's temper tantrums. I lost sight of creating a settlement to honor and respect the man I'd loved and instead focused on protecting myself.

I'd intended our divorce to be an offering to God. We prayed to be guided to the highest good. Even so, in the heat of debate, I forgot who I was. Luckily, I remembered Tosha, and asked her for help.

She responded:

"Here's what often works with folks who are divorcing. Just acknowledge that 100% of these assets belong to God, then ask to be shown the perfect settlement as *stewards* of the money, not the *owners*. It makes a world of difference. Once you completely offer everything to the Divine, the right actions will become clear. Your inner self will know what to do. Though your ego will argue that you should defend yourself, surrender actually has nothing to do with passivity. The act of offering often favors generosity and a win-win solution. But you don't have to figure it out; you'll be guided! Even if the Divine moves you to give more than the ego would like, don't forget. . . . She could replace that money ten times over, if it's Her Will."

As I considered her guidance, something tense and stuck relaxed inside me. My breath opened up. My shoulders dropped. I could feel the knot in my solar plexus give way.

Tosha continued:

"This can be hard to do. . . . But if you completely offer your assets to God, you'll be guided to the perfect settlement. You'll need to eliminate the word 'my' from your vocabulary. Instead of 'my money,' 'my house,' or even 'my daughter,' it's God's money, house, and little girl. Believing that all of these things belong to you is the ultimate illusion. I remind myself of this every day. If you do this, you'll feel like you dropped a huge weight, and a waterfall of abundance can come from places you never dreamed possible. You can do this, Lissa. It's your graduate school of surrender!"

Lightbulb moment.

I felt completely busted and humbled by my arrogance.

It was so clear, so obvious: I wanted God to choose how these blessings got distributed to serve the highest good. Though I felt so READY, I didn't know how to control my angry thoughts and impulses. My small self tended to take over with guarded, stingy, judgmental thoughts.

Tosha's advice:

"Don't beat up the small self for its tantrum; that's what small selves do, including mine. Just give that scared little kid a hug. She's simply frightened and feels threatened. Besides, you'll never get the small self to surrender; it doesn't know how to ask. Luckily you can ask God to do it through you with a Change Me Prayer."

So I did.

"Change me into someone who can surrender this to Divine Will without defending or grasping."

The minute I said it, I felt my heart open to this man I had loved for so long who had gifted me with the most beautiful daughter. My husband and I were finally able to look into each other's eyes for the first time in months.

The next mediation meeting became the last one. Our angry energy dissipated and we hammered out an agreement that felt generous to us both in half an hour! Within a month of negotiating our settlement, I got a large and unexpected royalty check—for exactly the amount I had agreed to pay in the settlement.

The story of my divorce is just one of many miracles I've experienced since choosing to live my life from a place of surrender. Tosha's book is chock full of stories like this.

Change Me Prayers will delight you, comfort you, make you laugh, and touch your heart. But it doesn't stop there. It shows you how to change from a person controlled by the ego to one through which the Divine can effortlessly flow. This wonderful book not only describes what can happen when you let the Divine take the lead, it also gives you the tools to make this a daily practice.

After lifetimes of letting the small self run your life, one finally comes to realize that it's just a hungry ghost. Even if you meet the love of your life, pursue meaningful work, earn plenty of money, and achieve everything "you" ever wanted, the ego will always want more. That's its nature.

But what CAN fill you completely is right here, right now, waiting to be let in.

If you're finally ready, Tosha's book will open you to receive this gift.

Lissa Rankin, M.D.

New York Times bestselling author
of *Mind Over Medicine*

Introduction

Someone wrote me once and said, "I LOVE your book *Outrageous Openness*, but I can't relate to these weird prayers you do. I don't *want* to change! It's taken me years to realize I'm *perfect* the way I am. Why on earth should I ask to be changed?"

Well, here's why. Yes, of *course* you are perfect as is, but is it possible you're still struggling? Einstein himself said that a problem could not be solved by the consciousness that created it. In other words, the ego can't solve the problems created by the ego!

It tries constantly to steer, often with great futility.

I'll tell you a deeply personal story about this.

I grew up incredibly close to my Pisces mom, Debby. She was my best friend; I was so bonded to her as a child, it was crazy. I remember when I was seven, she once left me watching cartoons. After about half-hour, I realized she wasn't home so I tore through the streets sobbing, certain she'd been kidnapped. But she'd gone next door to a neighbor for a cup of sugar.

When Mom and Dad went out on dates, my brothers would happily watch TV or romp with the babysitter. But I had my face pressed to the back window of the house,

1

counting the minutes until Mom's return, terrified there might be an accident.

What a poor, worried child!

Thank God I eventually became my own person, but my love for Mom never wavered. We talked almost every day for fifty years, often laughing until we cried. More than once we were hysterical, reminiscing about my ferocious attachment to her as a kid.

Two years ago I got the call I'd dreaded my whole life. My brother called to say that Mom, who was in her late eighties, was suddenly on her deathbed. How fast could I get there?

How could I do this? I knew in that moment that *I had no freakin' idea* how to say good-bye to the one Being on this planet I loved more than anything.

Believe me, I was well aware that no sanitized, pretty little affirmations like "I am open, safe, and relaxed" would have done a darn thing. I needed the Divine to take over and change me into One who could handle this.

So here is the prayer I used and the reason why this book exists.

Change me Divine Beloved into someone who can sit in this room and say good-bye to my beloved mom.

Change me into One who can watch her blessed body slide away.

Help me cry all I need and hand this ALL to You.

Allow me to know she is You and You can never leave me.

Let me let You take this over COMPLETELY.

So *that's* why I do these prayers. And they've carried me every step of the way.

All it takes is the invitation . . . and the offering. The Divine indeed can do what the small self never could.

✦

The essence of these prayers is surrender. You're inviting the Divine to make the changes IT wishes to make. But sometimes I hear from folks who use these to serve the ego's desires. However, here's the problem. If your longings are not offered to the Highest, they can create great distortion.

Once a woman named Gloria wrote me: "I love your work so I've dreamed up my own prayers to handle a mess I'm in. I fell in love with my next-door neighbor, Tim, but sadly, he's happily married to his wife. Then I realized I could do a prayer! So every day I say, "Change me God into a woman that Tim would leave his wife for. Make me into what he wants so we can be happy forever."

But oh my God, no, that's not what these are for! Their entire purpose is surrender to the Highest, the Divine will. Tim may not be meant for Gloria at all. Besides, these prayers, when clearly understood, allow for everyone's good, including the wife's.

Another prayer could save the day though. One like "Change me Divine into One who can offer all my attractions to you. Let me trust that the right relationship is already picked." Or even "Change me into One who knows all my needs are always met." That would address the issue without the ego taking control.

It takes practice to sense how to craft these, but over time it gets easier and easier.

What's amazing is how the Universe often knows precisely what's perfect for us, far beyond what we could imagine. We only need to make room to open and receive. The prayers in this book show how, such as this one:

> *Change me Divine Beloved into one who wants what You want for me. Let me trust that my needs will always be met in the Highest way when I allow You to guide me.*

✦

Someone wrote to me once on Facebook, where a big, funny community has sprung up around my writing, asking, "Hey what IS this? Are you running some kind of crazy religion or something?"

All I could say was, "Oh no, what a nightmare *that* would be!"

So no, I'm no guru, no savior, nada. I'm a writer, an imperfect Being, who simply fell in love with the Divine in my own heart. Anyone intensely motivated can do that. To me, *everyone* is a spark of Divinity, of Love Itself. Most of us just forget.

After spending half my life giving intuitive readings to folks around the world, I saw how most people chased the answers on the outside. I came to know we had to focus the lens within, where Love runs through our veins.

Then you no longer view the Universe as an ATM, a slot machine, or a shopping mall.

It becomes your willing and waiting Lover.

And hey, if *that's* a religion, well then, please, please sign me up.

Change me Divine Beloved into One who offers my whole Self to you with complete abandon.

   Let me forever serve You.

   Let me love and accept myself as You love me.

   May I find You shining brightly within my own Being.

DIVINE GUIDANCE

Divine Beloved, may I feel safe and guided by Your Love. Take over my body and mind, show me the way. Guide me always to the right actions at the right time. May I always feel immersed in Your Love, protected from fear and negativity.

Divine Beloved, let me only wish what You wish for me. May I see myself as You see me. Let me know my own Divinity in every moment. May I know I am You and may our desires be One.

May the Highest that is meant to happen, happen in me and through me.

May I be a vehicle for all You wish to occur.

Change me into One who can breathe, relax, and rest in Your arms.

1. Mise en Place

If you've ever read my work, you know by now that I consider almost nothing random.

If I'm cradling a question in my heart, to be shown the right direction I pay intense attention to the answers that come, no matter what delivery service God may use. License plates, billboards, songs on the radio, comments from strangers, all become grist for my own spiritual mill.

So my ears perked up like a Labrador one time when a stately, white-haired Frenchman turned to me in the produce aisle of the grocery store and exclaimed, "*Mise en place*, it's ALL about *mise en place, n'est-ce pas*? It's the consummate key!"

I nodded and thanked him, though I had no idea what the hell he was talking about. I made a note to check when I got home, but if you're a cook, you may already know.

I discovered *mise en place* is a French phrase for prepping all the ingredients for a meal: getting everything washed, chopped, and in order. Some people would even include cleaning and readying the kitchen. That way, when it's time, you can cook with abandon.

Well, I couldn't think of a better message. I could feel

in my bones that a big wave of new life was lurking right around the bend.

So get ready! Clean out the closets, finish up loose ends, get rid of what needs to go. Create a vacuum for the New to fill. Release dead weight, old destructive habits, exhausting relationships. Pick a few items off the procrastination list and whisk them away.

And if the Divine wants to make a delicious meal out of you, well, you'll be prepared.

Change me Divine Beloved into One who easily releases all that's ready to go, making room for what wants to come. May I courageously release all that is outgrown and stagnant, preparing for the new. Let me move in harmony with Your natural cycles in every way.

2. Jailbreak

The other day, I bumped into my old pal Jon at Whole Foods. "Tosha," he beamed, grabbing my arm, "don't you write self-help books these days?"

I gave him a long, quizzical look, and since the line stretched all the way back to the kombucha aisle, I launched into an explanation.

"Well, not quite self-help. To me, that's like redecorating a prison cell. You know, change that ugly couch, hang new curtains, maybe add a nice shag rug. For a bonus we'll even show you how to attract that right partner to serve your sentence with!"

Jon chuckled.

"But letting the Divine lead is a whole other deal. You surrender to Love. You're actually taken over . . ."

(On that note, I wondered if I sounded like some evangelical kook, but actually Jon was listening with rapt attention. So I forged on, as the line slowly made its way to the cookie counter.)

"You know, a lot of self-help is about getting a new, improved ego. Making wishes come true. It's like those 'I Want More' conferences you hear about. But why rely on fulfilling the limited ego and its endless desires? Why not let Something Bigger take over?"

As we finally got to the cash register, Jon's eyes lit up.

"Yes, I got it," he said, giving me a hug. "It's the difference between redecorating that prison cell or . . . walking out the door."

"Yes!" I answered.

And then we both did.

> *Change me Divine Beloved into One who always remembers my true nature. Wake me from the trance of separation from You. Use me according to Your will as a force of love on the planet.*

3. Kick It to the Curb

Someone wrote me a letter once that said, "Many, many horrible things have happened to me. So when you say 'God never gives you more than you can handle,' I want to spit!"

Well, I really understand that feeling. I can even sympathize. The New Age and even spiritual worlds can be filled with cold, simplistic clichés that make my eyes roll. But here's what took me a long time to figure out.

The idea isn't, "God never gives you more than the ego can handle." Being born with an anxious mind, I used to live in a daily state of terror until I learned the kind of Divine focus I teach. My mind made my life a walking hell. No amount of therapy "fixed" it.

So the critical concept really is, "God never gives you more than you can handle IF YOU INCLUDE AND INVITE THE DIVINE." And that creates a whole other galaxy!

But it takes practice.

You learn to also embrace the ups and downs of prarabdha karma, the curriculum that each individual soul came to learn in a given lifetime. You have deep inner support as you navigate that road and stop seeing God as a mean-spirited Force that flings hardship and travail your way.

So yes, I do know what you mean. Luckily, this Divine

route is very different from "trying to get the ego to adapt to and survive" challenges. Rather it's a profound invitation, an offering, which casts the burden of problems to this Force of Love. It's often born of desperation. But if you learn to truly do it, again and again, your life is *never* the same.

And anyway, what do you have to lose? Only anger, fear, and a sense of victimization, all such a big relief to kick to the curb.

> *Change me Divine Beloved into One who can easily invite You into all matters, big or small. Share this life, permeate my understanding. Allow my awareness to be One with Your own in every way.*

4. Thinking Outside the Tub

I spent one December in Guanajuato, Mexico, in a Spanish immersion program, staying in a funky hostel by the school. While my room was sunny, it had no heat, and this mountain town was in a serious cold snap. I went to sleep each night in five layers of clothing and four blankets, counting my visible breaths like fluffy sheep, in Spanish, for practice.

On the second day I was thrilled to notice there was a huge tile tub in the bathroom, bigger than any I'd ever seen. I hatched a plan: I would warm up each night by running a hot bath, then dash like mad into bed before I cooled off.

But that evening I saw that there was only enough hot water to fill the tub three measly inches. Then it would turn icy. Did that stop me? No, I just lay in my shallow hot pool, barely covering my ankles and fingers while the rest of my body froze.

You know how they say insanity is doing the same thing over and over, expecting a different result? Each night I filled this same munchkin-sized pool, anticipating more hot water. And each night I got out colder than I began.

After a week, I surrendered. I asked, "Okay, really, God, what am I missing here? If You want me to survive the month, You gotta show me what to do . . . or at least send a bathtub miracle."

That evening, in a blinding flash of insight that would have been obvious to any toddler, I finally saw the tub was meant to be . . . a shower. Bliss rained down if I stepped in as soon as the water heated, and jumped out when it ended.

Five full minutes of nightly shower joy came as soon as I released my fixed ideas.

And then I found out I could ask for a space heater, but that's a different story.

> *Change me Divine Beloved into One who can*
> *embrace Reality. Help me release fixed and*
> *stubborn ideas and invite Divine solutions.*
> *Open and expand my mind. I am Yours!*

5. When Begging Ends

I love the idea of Divine Source. It reminds us that every-thing, the fulfillment of every need, always emanates from the One. So if you learn how to keep your vibration high and attuned to That, whatever is needed to sustain you can always occur, often in surprising and delightful ways. Your Source is never a particular person, place, or thing, but God Herself. You never have to beg.

Furthermore, Divine Source says that whatever reso-nates with you will always find you. That which does not, will fall away.

It's that simple.

When *Outrageous Openness* first came out, I experi-enced this as I took the book around—some stores were simply not drawn to it. But knowing about Divine Source and resonance, I didn't care.

I remember taking it to a spiritual bookstore in down-town San Francisco. The desultory manager sort of half-growled, "Oh, we have a long, long wait here. You can leave a copy for our 'pile' in the back room. Then you could call a ton and plead with us. If you get lucky, maybe one day we'll stock it. Just keep hoping."

"Oh, my God, no!" I shuddered. "Why would I keep twisting your arm? It'll go easily to the places that are right. You never have to convince someone. The people who are right will just know."

He looked stunned when I thanked him, smiling, and left.

And sure enough, other store clerks were so excited, even from the cover alone. They nearly ripped the book out of my hands as I walked in. When I brought it to the main bookstore in San Francisco's Castro district, I noticed the manager striding toward me was wearing a baseball cap with an image of the goddess Lakshmi.

"Great sign," I mused.

He held the book for a second without even cracking it open, then showed the cover to a coworker, yelling, "Hey, let's give this baby a coming-out party!"

So a few weeks later, they did. Sake, fortune cookies, and all.

Because you see, what's meant for you will always, always find you. You never have to be bothered by the people who aren't meant to understand. And anyway, sometimes years later, they are ready . . . and they do.

Change me Divine Beloved into One who knows that You alone are my Source. Let me trust that You fling open every door at the right time. Free me from the illusion of rejection, competition, and scarcity. Fill me with confidence and faith, knowing I never have to beg, just gratefully receive.

6. Who Saves Your Butt?

You never know who might arrive . . . and when. I was thinking about this as I finished the stories for this book, since every step of this manuscript I've been getting editing help from my best friend, Amy, from upstate New York.

She dropped into my life out of nowhere many years ago in the empty parking lot behind a yoga center. She had overheard me say I was driving to Manhattan, so she just knocked on my window and asked to jump in! I was like, who IS this petite, wacky artist in the wire-rim glasses and turquoise cap?

Twenty-five years later she's editing all my books. Honestly, she's like my behind-the-scenes secret weapon; everyone needs another set of eyes that can catch what you might miss. I know God sent her because she not only has one of the most creative, divergent minds I've ever encountered—as well as a kind and generous heart—but she can also make me laugh until I wet my pants. For someone like me, that's sort of critical.

She makes me think of the incredible ways the Universe sends help if you are truly open and willing. I didn't go looking for her; she jumped in my freakin' car! Every day I feel such gratitude for her.

So who do you appreciate? You never know when your own Amy might walk up and knock on your own window . . . if you're open.

Change me Divine Beloved into One who is willing to receive ALL the right help, knowing each person, animal, or thing is a form of You. Let me feel deserving of Divine assistance in every way. Open me to receive.

7. Chasing Chihuahuas

One day I was writing on the sunny deck of Peet's in Berkeley when all HELL broke loose. A lady tied her black Great Dane to a folding chair and went inside for a drink.

Suddenly the poor dog was mesmerized by a cute passing Chihuahua and took off like a rocket, dragging the chair with him down the street. Absolute and complete canine cacophony. Thank heavens someone quickly freed him.

I was sitting there thinking, "Lady, this might be a really, really good moment to ask God to show you what size object to tie your horse to next time."

I do think there's a spiritual lesson here about *viveka*, the Sanskrit word for mental discrimination. Yet I sure didn't judge her. Who hasn't done something cuckoo like this?

I actually sat there bemused, wondering who I related to more, the lady or the dog.

At times it's a toss-up.

*Change me Divine Beloved into One who allows
You to guide my mind and life in every way.
Keep me focused and centered, so right actions
may occur. Guide me in harmony with the
Way. Release me from the grip of distractions,
trusting You always bring whatever I need.*

8. Special Offer

One day I got this email:

"Hi, Tosha,

"Wouldn't you like to join our special program to give you EXTRA-mystical kundalini so you can develop Divine Super Powers? This is a one-time offer you don't want to miss! Only $99 a month and you'll learn how to make everything you could EVER want happen!"

Um . . . let me think.

Okay, how about, "Absolutely not!"

I figure that the Divine One who owns me takes care of everything. If I needed those powers He'd sure as heck bring them. But why would I WANT them? I let Him bring what He wants His own way without invasive manipulations on my end.

The truth is if you trust God implicitly you don't need to hunt for anything like this. In fact, you'd run for the hills. So many people develop these powers from a sense of fear or scarcity. Actually, the Hindu scriptures have a lot to say about focusing on the Divine Beloved rather than developing siddhis or powers like these. It can be a detour or even spiritual prison.

Thanks an awful lot for the exciting offer though.

*Change me Divine Beloved into One who
trusts all needs are always met. Let me align
myself completely with Your will. Free me
from any wish to manipulate outcomes,
knowing I naturally attract the Highest in every
moment, just by my Oneness with You.*

9. Wildly Open to the New

Back in my twenties, I took classes with a psychic who gave one steady piece of advice. He would say, "Do Something New each day. Even if you just use your left hand rather than your right or go to a different café." He insisted that by simply doing this, we would reanimate the brain, break patterns, and kick open energy.

To this day, whenever I feel stuck or depressed, I use his advice.

Once I did this for a week. I finally started that salsa class I'd been procrastinating about for five years, then the next day wrote in the park rather than in my usual spots. I cleaned a certain closet I'd been resisting forever and even took a long-delayed hike up Mount Wittenberg. By the end of the week I was so energized, I showed up at a friend's party rather than hiding away writing, as usual.

She was in shock.

It was all so uplifting, and you can see why. Grooves get cut deep into the mind from endless repetition of patterns, so habit can keep us imprisoned in ways we don't even notice. Sometimes a simple game of "something new" can shift neural patterning quickly.

So tie your shoelaces the opposite way. Eat something

novel. Talk to someone you wouldn't normally notice. If you start to think, "I'm not the kind of person who . . . ," drop that for now.

And pretend.

Fixed patterns and identities start dissolving, everything starts unsticking.

Find out where the Divine will actually lead you if that wall of resistance isn't in the way.

Change me Divine Beloved into One who is wildly open to the New. Grant me the willingness to experiment and play. Free me from rigid patterns that no longer serve. Let me feel adventurous and spontaneous, knowing that the more I open to life, the more it opens to me.

10. Process of Illumination

Once I was sitting in a quiet, secluded spot in the woods of Marin when suddenly I heard the most supernal, otherworldly sound.

Someone was playing a cello.

My whole being surrendered as I absorbed the spontaneous gift of a Bach suite in the middle of the forest, in the middle of nowhere. It was as if there was no player at all, just an instrument igniting like a flame, offering its sound with abandon to the trees, birds, wind, Eternity.

Total stillness.

Then bird calls resumed.

A few crackling branches, rustling leaves.

I could hear the musician and his friend's muffled talk.

The friend said, "Oh, my God! You never sounded like this before. What happened?"

The cellist laughed and answered softly, "I lived in hell a long, long time. I lost—to be honest—everything. Money, marriage, home, the music. Almost my sanity. Everything.

"Things returned but now it's all different. Perhaps I've been humbled.

"The Music does as it wishes."

*Change me Divine Beloved into One who can
get out of the way. Release me, open me. Let
me be a pure, clear conduit for Your Love.*

11. The Jewel-Studded Wheel

A dream: I'm on a boat with a large, gorgeous steering wheel studded with sapphires, amethysts, and pearls. I'm gripping it tightly, trying to steer. I'm taking the job seriously, since the boat is huge and we're navigating a tight canal. But to be honest, no matter how I spin that thing, it sure doesn't seem to affect much.

Eventually a tall, elegant Japanese woman walks over and says, "Hey, didn't anyone tell you? That wheel is just for show; it's decoration. We all love how you're trying to make it work, but on this boat, the steering actually happens from the back. You might as well go have some fun. Nothing you're doing up here matters even one bit."

I burst out laughing and wake up.

Still laughing.

> *Change me Divine Beloved into One who happily allows You to steer in every way. I invite You to take the lead. Help me release the need to control outcomes; take my fear of letting go. I am Yours, You are Mine, all is well.*

DIVINE WORTH

Divine Beloved, change me into One who every day remembers who I REALLY am—a living, breathing conduit for Love.

May I wake up to who I actually AM:

All I encounter.

May I be carried by Divine Grace in every moment.

May I know my true nature as Love itself.

12. Out with God

I know a guy named Pat who from a young age always sensed he was gay. But he grew up in a strict, southern fundamentalist family so coming out felt impossible. Hiding his true self had caused him such heartbreak and stress, he'd developed a ferocious red rash all over his body.

When he turned twenty, he finally succumbed to his family's pressure and went to a singles dance at their church. His mom kept insisting he hadn't met the right girl yet.

What a nightmare! At the dance, he felt like a cyborg from another planet. As he was leaving, a kind woman from church noticed his despair and asked if she could help. Pat admitted it was a horrible night, and that he felt totally alienated. The woman looked at him with intense blue eyes and shared a secret.

She'd long been in an empty marriage where she'd never been content. The real twist was that she and her next-door neighbor, another devoted church lady, had fallen in love years before. They still practiced their religion but felt crushed by its inherent homophobia, and were plotting to flee to a larger, more accepting town.

She begged Pat to be honest while he was still young and not lose half his life as she had, living a lie.

Luckily, the story has a happy ending. The two church women eventually escaped to the open-minded haven of Atlanta. Pat crashed at their new home until he could find roots.

Recently he confided that although his family had disowned him, he still hoped they'd one day relent. Meanwhile he had become a barista at a café, found his first boyfriend, and gotten his first tattoo.

And there was no rash in sight.

He was thrilled to be living the way he was made.

> *Change me Beloved into One who has the courage to be my true self. Let me honor my authenticity just as I am. Allow me to honor my sexuality, desires, and needs as sacred expressions of Your Divine Love.*

13. God Is Funk

To me, music is one of the endlessly compelling forms of the Divine. But with all my Aquarius, I could never have a narrow view of so-called spiritual music. I figure if it moves you, comforts you, or just makes you fly, that's plenty.

How could God NOT be present in something that makes you feel that way?

Once a woman called me who had been a resident of a meditation community for years. She said the group had strict ideas of "dharmic" music. Certain chants and bhajans were considered godly, while everything else was considered profane. Then she confessed her own guilty secret: Each day she eagerly awaited the moment when she could flee to the privacy of her Subaru and rock out to the Stones. She was so paranoid other members would see her that she drove several miles before she cranked up the volume and went totally, unabashedly out of control.

Under absolutely nobody's thumb.

I told her I considered that tripped-out time in her car to be as profound and sacred as anything else in her day. It held the mystical essence of How God Had Created Her to Be Uniquely Herself.

Why should she pretend to be anything else?

So I've been drawn forever to vinyasa yoga classes that play hip-hop, jazz, funk, bluegrass, punk, or rock as often as chanting.

And while Handel's Messiah might make me cry, in certain moods so will Marvin Gaye, Lorde, or k.d. lang.

Change me Beloved into One who embraces my own uniqueness, knowing You come in countless ways. Let me accept my own nature completely, knowing it, too, is Divine. May I love myself as I am, not as others say I should be.

14. You Want Me to Do What?

I used to know this great woman, Maggie, very New Jersey Italian. I learned a lot from being around her. She had a huge heart coupled with a healthy sense of self-respect. When someone made a particularly odd demand she'd say, "Wait, wait, you want me to do . . . WHAT?"

Sometimes she'd even ask the person to repeat it.

Then she'd pause a long time as if she were actually really considering deeply. Finally she'd say emphatically, "Um . . . no. That WON'T be happening," and burst into peals of laughter until she almost fell out of her chair.

If you grew up in a situation without boundaries, you may find the Divine sends certain situations *just* to give you the pleasure of saying *no* . . . and realizing, gratefully, that you are no longer six.

What a delight.

> *Change me Beloved into One who easily sets boundaries wherever needed. May I feel entitled to say no to any situation that feels bad or wrong. Fill me with Divine confidence, speak through me.*

15. Take the High Road

Once on a hiking trail I overheard an astonishing conversation. Two women about the same age were chatting behind me.

One said, "Yep, my thirty-third birthday is tomorrow. And y' know, it's ALL downhill from here. I mean, I'll never be this young or hot again. Everything's gonna get harder and harder. Each year there'll be less chance for love, adventure, work. Decrepitude's just around the next bend."

I peeked over my shoulder and spotted her friend nodding somberly in agreement, blonde ponytail bobbing. "So true!" she said, her brow furrowed with concern. "The game'll pretty much be over in a couple more years. Better flaunt it while we got it!"

As they passed by, I couldn't help but surreptitiously scan both their faces for traces of irony or humor. But oh, my God, no, I couldn't believe it. They honestly weren't joking. I was flummoxed.

I mean, they were completely wrong in so many different ways. They had taken a megadose of all the toxic thoughts of scarcity, fear, and loss embedded in this culture, most especially for women.

Because the truth is, our reality is deeply etched by

HOW we see it, and by the limiting thoughts habitually formed in our minds. Think your life is over at thirty-five and you can indeed build a wall of constriction and fear that's a self-fulfilling prophecy.

But believe that you're barely getting started (I tell myself that each day) and the Divine can bring miracles beyond anything the ego can imagine. THAT becomes your daily reality instead.

It's all how you hold your vibration . . . and your mind.

Change me Beloved into One who knows my Spirit is eternal and ageless. Let me release any old ideas of constriction or limitation, returning to my true essence as expansive, radiant Light. My whole Being is filled with joy, energy, and beauty, a vessel for the Divine Shakti.

16. The Benefits of Being Ignored

One day I was in Valencia with my friend Jen, when I saw a bag in the window of a small shop. It was the right size for my laptop so I went in to find out the price, since it wasn't marked.

Well, I'll bet you've had this happen. The sales gal was animatedly chatting with someone, and when she looked over at me, she held up a finger like, "Wait." And then went back to her conversation . . . about the Coachella Music Festival . . . Beck's guitar playing . . . Outkast . . . on and on.

After a minute, Jen was furious. "WHY are you waiting?" she hissed, "she's SO rude! She's just ignoring you!"

But here's the thing. Life gets pretty darn interesting if you don't always take this stuff personally. So I figured the Divine was saying there was another, better plan, that's all.

We left.

And went across the street to a charity consignment store that raises money for AIDS.

The guy behind the counter greeted us with an unusually friendly hello.

And right *there*, in that funky shop, was the exact *same* bag, different color, this time with the original tags even still on. "Where on earth did you get this?" I asked, astonished.

"Oh, someone bought it across the street, but changed her mind and they won't take returns. They're pretty snooty." He grinned. "So she donated it to us. Do you want it?"

Um . . . YES!!

And I got it for just a few bucks that went to a good charity. A much better plan.

So that's how the Divine can drag you around with even the smallest stuff.

Besides you never, ever have to beg for attention. If someone is pointedly ignoring you, it may mean the Universe is saying that you're headed the wrong way. Go where you're welcome and an unexpected door may fly dramatically open.

God may even have a whole new bag for you.

Change me Divine Beloved into One who knows that every door that needs to open always will. Release me from the illusion that I need to beg for attention. Make me receptive to all miracles and surprises as I let You lead the way.

17. The Dumbest Idea

About seven years ago the ideas that became *Outrageous Openness* were beginning to percolate inside. But I had no idea whatsoever how they could turn into a book. I just knew it was a message that wanted to get out.

I heard there would soon be a publishing conference in downtown San Francisco. Once a year a team came from the big houses in New York, and you'd get five minutes to "pitch" your stuff to them. (This was really before DIY took off so hugely.) So I bought my seventy-five-dollar ticket and trotted down there. Little did I know at the time how useless most of these events could be. But I figured what the heck, the Universe could use anything.

I can still remember entering the cavernous, fluorescent-lit conference room at the Hyatt. There were a zillion hopeful writers there, all waiting patiently and nervously in line for their "moment" with a rep. I was so clueless about it all, I just showed up thinking if a miracle was meant to be, it would happen.

I listened while the guy in front of me pitched a story about a dinosaur couple who had a wedding. After eating and killing a lot of people. Yes. He. Did.

I could overhear encouraging words from the rep like, "Hey, keep going, man. GREAT idea. Yes . . . BIG market! HUGE! HUGE! Send me a few pages soon!" He handed dino-guy his card with a beaming smile and a pat on the back.

Then it was me.

I tried to quickly explain this idea about letting the Divine Take the Lead instead of pushing, forcing, or manifesting. The rep listened to me quietly for about two minutes.

Then he held up his hand like a stop sign and scrunched his face as if he had a hernia. "Oh, my God, *no more*. No more, I don't need more. But I hafta tell ya. I've been doing these for ten years and that is honestly the DUMBEST idea I've ever heard. Ever! Hey, no offense, okay?"

The he gestured dramatically to the person behind me. "Next!"

Which all goes to show, even if someone thinks something is the absolute worst idea in the world, but God *wants* it to happen and if it is offered over entirely—it indeed *will*.

Same goes for you.

Just don't listen.

Change me Divine Beloved into One who offers all actions and projects over to You alone. Let me trust that if something is meant to be, it will always BE, regardless of criticism or ridicule. May I always stay true to my inspiration, regardless of the opinions of others. May I trust where You are guiding me, knowing that doors open at the right time as needed when You are my Source.

18. Not All Good

Someone wrote me once, "So how do you know *when* to flow and when to say No? I used to have an abusive husband. Was I supposed to just flow with that?"

No, no, of course not.

If you offer the dilemma over to the Divine, you're shown the right action from the inside. Then the next thing to do arises organically from your own body.

Your instincts *show* you. It's not a rigid set of rules, or a formula.

When *Outrageous Openness* first came out, I was invited to read at a Northern California hot springs. They confirmed the date and requested many boxes of books. So I packed up the Prius and spent several hours shlepping there.

Well, when I arrived, they had forgotten and booked someone else. And I was even mostly rolling with that until I asked that they simply apologize for the trouble.

But the director demurred. "Hey, your book is on 'letting go and letting God.' You shouldn't care. It's *all good*, right?"

Well, *that* made me momentarily crazy.

Because spirituality doesn't mean you completely disrespect other people's time and energy and then say, "Just let go. It was your karma. No problema."

And besides, spirituality doesn't mean you never get mad! Believe me, if you have a bunch of fire planets and a strong Pluto like me, you do get mad sometimes. You don't have to be a robot.

When emotions are offered to the Divine, they can be honored . . . and then released. You can send love to the hurt, scared, or angry parts of yourself. You don't have to beat yourself up for having feelings in the first place. They come like a thunderstorm, or a gentle warm spring rain . . . and then they go.

They're not "you."

So I've long since forgiven that wacky, disorganized place. I even still visit there often because their waters are serene and beautiful. That's *aparagraha*, the Sanskrit word for nongrasping and release. I'm happy to support them.

At the same time, unless they offer apologies or amends, I'd never do an event there again. That's just healthy self-respect and boundaries. No need get run over by the same tractor-trailer twice.

Because sometimes going with the flow just means saying . . . *hell no.*

Change me Divine Beloved into One who honors my emotions. Let me have my feelings without judgment, and then release them. May I feel deserving to say no when needed. Show me how to be kind and loving to the child inside who needs care.

19. Tao of Barbie

I grew up, like many girls (and a few boys), entranced with Barbie. In fact, a huge part of my childhood in small-town Pennsylvania was spent dressing, undressing, and re-dressing her absurdly disproportionate body with every kind of clothing imaginable. All to get ready for her endless dates with Ken . . . or Skipper.

(Yes, I also sent her out with an androgynously dressed Skipper, pretending they weren't sisters. "Why can she only date *Ken?*" I would ask my poor mom, who could only roll her eyes. Years later she would see Rachel Maddow on MSNBC and finally, finally understand.)

Anyway, I digress. The truth is I had a total love/hate story with that glamour doll.

On the one hand, Barbie was compelling, fueling a passion for fashion that's never abated, letting me adore Cher and RuPaul with equal fervor. While I took the heads off regular baby dolls ("I'm not diapering anything!" I'd yell, a true Plutonic child), this ravishing plastic clothing queen could keep me mesmerized for hours.

On the other hand, who knows what self-hatred and eating disorders were fueled by having her as a role model?

Many a feminist Ph.D. thesis has been written about Barbie's destructive effect on girls' self-image.

Amazing how few women in this culture feel acceptance for their bodies just as they are. Almost everyone wishes to be thinner, younger, or just . . . different. Self-rejection is rampant. Reclaiming one's own body as beautiful, sexy, and right no matter how it matches narrow cultural standards is radical indeed.

For me, this shift came in my early thirties when I recovered from a collapse of my adrenal system. I wrote in *Outrageous Openness* that I'd been bedridden for almost three years after Western doctors said I'd never recover. Then a gifted acupuncturist healed me. I eventually felt such gratitude to have a body that could do the most basic things, like walk or swallow food, I never judged myself the old way again. I was just so darn grateful to have a working body, I could care less that it didn't match photos in magazines.

It became easy to appreciate the body for its highest purpose: as a vehicle for the Divine, as a way to know God within your own cells.

Thank heavens anyone can apply this awareness . . . even a diehard Barbie-lover.

Change me Divine Beloved into One who accepts my body exactly as it is, seeing it as a vessel for Your love. Let me know myself as a spark of Divinity. Fill me with gratitude for this physical form. Let me nurture and care for myself in every way.

20. *The Tyranny of "Should"*

Yesterday I was crossing Telegraph Avenue after yoga when I ran into my friend Becky. While I usually see her dancing through a graceful vinyasa, this time she looked like a ball of nerves. Her round, open face was streaked with tears; she even seemed embarrassed to see me. I hugged her and asked, "Need to talk?"

We sat down at a café. Turned out she was in the middle of a romantic drama, attracted to her work supervisor and fretting like mad. She admitted she was driving herself bonkers.

But here's what really struck me.

Despite her fixation, Becky's problem wasn't her crush . . . but how she blamed herself. She kept saying, "I *shouldn't* be going through this. I'm a yoga teacher, for Christ sake. Yet here I am, driven wild by romance like I'm twelve! What's *wrong* with me?"

I sympathized. How often I've heard this sort of self-blame from my cosmic pals. "I've meditated for ten years, I should be enlightened by now." "I've taken five intensives, I should never lose my cool." "I'm open to the Divine, so I should never, ever be lonely."

But why? Where do these ideas come from? They're

painful self-torture from a destructive culture of competition; just new ways for the ego to spank itself. They're spiritualized versions of other "shoulds," like needing to be the smallest dress size or getting the biggest paycheck.

Yet all growth and healing comes from one thing: love.

Luckily there's an easy way out. Send love to the part that's hurting.

After all, that's what it's crying for.

"So what if this attraction to your boss *is* your route to God right now?" I asked. "Why blame yourself? Is this any less spiritual than standing on your head? Once it's okay to feel whatever you feel you can relax. Can you send yourself acceptance and let it be okay that you feel the attraction? I mean, really, you don't have to do anything more about it right now than that.

And then . . . *que sera, sera!*"

> *Change me Divine Beloved into One who*
> *can love myself in every condition. Free me*
> *from self-torture. Fill me to my core with self-*
> *acceptance and worthiness. Let me allow and*
> *honor ALL my feelings, however they arise.*
> *Wherever I am, guide my way. I am Yours.*
> *You are Mine. We are One. All is well.*

21. The Inner Kiss

My friend Dan is a long-distance cyclist who's had painful bouts of sciatica since he was a teen. No practitioner has been able to help him heal. Each time a recurrence flares, he blames himself more, furious that he can't work out.

He once asked me, "Have you ever noticed how only humans blame ourselves for our wounds? If an animal gets hurt, it'll go into a corner and lick itself till it's better. If it's traumatized, it'll tremble to release the tension. But a person in our nutty culture will beat himself up for being hurt in the first place.

"If I had a dog with a lame foot, would I hit it for not walking right? Yet I do that to myself all the time."

I so agreed. Mostly we're taught to curse our hurt spot, but we each have one! In astrology, it's called the Chiron point, the weak link that each of us carries into a given life. It might be about self-worth, love, money, health, whatever.

So I suggested that Dan could send love to his condition. Just *love* it. Kiss it, embrace it. Bow to it. Offer it to the Divine. It's desperate for acceptance; the body is always just trying to do the best that it can with what it has. And no matter how much love comes from the outside, Chiron can only be healed from within.

I asked, "Haven't you been around a kid who's skinned his knee and wanted you to kiss and make it better? Well, I figure we're all just waiting for that Inner Kiss."

He grinned. "So if I accept it, will the freakin' sciatica finally go away?"

I said, "You know, if it's meant to heal it may finally do so, because you won't be beating yourself with anger. Your body will be inundated with love. But the real point is the self-acceptance either way. 'Cause once you willingly embrace that seemingly broken part, you become whole."

Besides, animals and children always know best, right?

Change me Divine Beloved into One who can send love to my injuries and wounds. Let me accept myself totally just as I am. Help me care for and accept my body as it is, knowing it's always doing the best it can. May I be an ally and friend to my beloved body. Let me love others that way, too.

22. God as Fashion Police: Just Be You

So Atria, my publisher, decided they wanted to use *Outrageous Openness* as one of their first books for an online video course. One week their video crew came to my place for the wild ride of filming it.

Actually it was a lot of fun. But what really tickled me was the stuff about clothes.

I had to decide between two dresses. One was conservative and honestly, not really me. But to its credit, it did cover my tattoos. The other was wilder. So I asked the Divine to choose, then my Capricorn went and put on the more conventional one (only because I didn't want to give more conservative viewers in Oklahoma or Idaho a nervous breakdown while they examined my arms).

Then I ran off to a café and accidentally poured tea all over the damn thing.

Laughing, I raced home to change into the other one.

Clearly the Universe had an opinion.

When the producer, Gail, arrived, I told her what happened and she said, "But of course we'd want you to be yourself! Love the dress. Oh, and the tats!"

That just made me laugh. And if you think about it, it's plumb crazy. I mean, why the heck would you write a book called OUTRAGEOUS Openness in the first place and then put on some tame, restrained little dress?

So just go be You today, okay?

Even I forget at certain moments . . . then God has to swat me a bit.

> *Change me Divine Beloved into One who can easily and joyfully embrace myself just as I am, as You made me. Let me enjoy my own uniqueness and individuality, being my full, unbridled Self—tastes, preferences, and all. May I love myself as You love me.*

23. The Spark You Are

Never forget you are Eternity Itself pretending at times to be a worried, fearful, or sometimes cranky human. You are a spark of unlimited Divinity. You are expansive Light encased in form.

So whenever someone says, "What do you expect? I'm only *human*!" I often laugh and think, "You are?"

> *Change me O Divine Beloved into One who always remembers my true identity: unlimited Light and Love. Let me know myself as pure Consciousness. Wake me from the sleepwalk of believing I am "only" human.*
>
> *I am Yours. You are Mine. We are One.*

DIVINE PROSPERITY

May I always trust the Divine Flow.
   May I always know there is Enough.
   Change me into One who always trusts You.
   Change me into One who feels worthy to
open to true Abundance.

24. Urvelcm

One time in Los Angeles I stopped at a random jeweler to replace a dead watch battery. It was a packed-to-the-gills tiny shop off Fairfax Avenue. The guy behind the counter turned out to be an ancient European Jew who spoke in a heavy Yiddish accent just like my grandpa Zede.

He started joking around the minute I walked in. "So vhy you abuse dis watch to make battery die?"

"Oh, yes, every day I throw it on the ground!" I bantered back.

"Vell, at least you don't throw at people!"

"Well, sometimes I throw it at cars."

His eyes twinkled. "Vell den, you should throw only at rich people's cars."

Wow. That made me pause.

"Why?" I asked.

He looked serious. "Zhey don't make you angry?"

"Why would they?" I asked, truly curious. "Anyway, how do you know *I'm* not rich?"

"You?" he said, rolling his eyes dramatically. "I see dat beat-up Prius. Dat crazy handbag with the bird feathers you carry. No Prada, no Gucci. YOU? *You're* not rich." Now he was snorting with laughter.

"But honestly, I always feel I am," I confessed. "If you know that God will always bring what you need, then you're rich. If you don't trust that, then you're not. It's definitely NOT what's in the bank."

"You a little meshuga," he answered, scratching his beard and peering at me over his wire-rim glasses. "But . . . very, very interesting! Today I tink about dis all day. *Zei Gezunt!*"

And he smiled, handing me back my fixed watch.

I walked out the door, inwardly thanking the Divine for the conversation. And then, no joke. A car with *this* license plate drove by a minute later: URVELCM

> *Change me Divine Beloved into One who knows You alone are the source of all prosperity. Let me live in gratitude, trusting every need is handled and always will be. Release me from the prison of jealousy, knowing whatever is meant for me always comes. That alone is true wealth.*

25. Cool Cop

Yesterday I got my first speeding ticket in twenty years, for going thirty-five in a twenty-five zone. But at least the cop was engaging. How often does *that* happen?

She pulled me over and yelled, in an amused Bronx accent, the name on my plate, "Hey, KaliKar. You ready? 'Cause I'm sooo totally about to loove ruining your day."

After she wrote the ticket, she actually said, "Well, listen. Just take this baby home, pay it, and don't waste a minute being mad. Yeh, yeh, it's gonna be pricey. Like three hundred smackeroos pricey. But it's ALL your attitude . . . if you trust there'll be more where this came from, there WILL be."

Wow, excuse me? A cop giving abundance advice so eerily similar to my own? I have to admit I was charmed by the wild serendipity of it all. Besides, you never know *what* karma is getting resolved by an event. The message to slow down was not lost during a week when I was juggling far too much.

In the end, I admitted that she'd made the ticket about as much fun as a debacle like this could be. She said, "Well look, I've been doing this a long time. I want you to have a good day whether you gotta deal with me or not."

I smiled. "Well, if you wanted it that badly you could've just given me a warning."

She winked, "Nah, darlin'. I didn't want it THAT bad."

Driving away, she yelled out the window, "Till we meet again, KaliKar. Stop bein' in such a hurry cuz I'll be watchin'."

Okay, then. How many cops can give you an expensive ticket but still leave you laughing by the side of the road?

Change me Divine Beloved into One who can roll with what cannot change, grateful even for hard knocks. Let me embrace all tests whenever they come. And may I release any fear of financial loss, knowing that all can be replenished with ease by Divine Will.

26. Half-Empty Glass

Last night my neighbor Mary and I ran into each other in the hall of our apartment building. Since we're both rabid cyclists, we often chat during these impromptu meetings but never get far.

You see, Mary is a devout pessimist, and I, for better or worse, with three planets in fiery Sag, am an irrepressible optimist. Despite our shared biking passion, after ten minutes we've usually ridden straight into a ditch.

So I mentioned I'd been training to do the AIDS fundraising ride from San Francisco down to LA, something I'd considered forever. Mary rolled her eyes.

"The AIDS ride? Don't you need like three thousand dollars in donations for that? Who'd give anything to you in an economy like this?"

"You know," I said, smiling, "if my gut says do it, one way or another the money will come. It'll just happen."

"Nice fantasy," Mary said, glancing at her watch. "Seriously, do you live on Planet Fairydust? You seem to enjoy pretending a lot."

"But my whole life's been one long string of coincidences," I protested. "Even in dark times. They all just came from being, well . . . wide open."

"Yeah, whatever," Mary said, shaking her head. "Well, g'night."

To be honest, I think my adventurous *joie de vivre* drives Mary kinda nuts. Another time we ran into each other when I was returning from a spontaneous road trip. When she asked where I'd gone, I said that I'd driven off with a suitcase, food, and a credit card, simply open to seeing where I'd be guided. I'd ended up having the best week, heading down the California coastline to the desert of Palm Springs.

"Are you insane?" she snickered. "Without reservations or plans? I did stuff like that when I was eighteen but . . ."

"Yep." I chuckled. "For some of us, it doesn't really change."

"Well, good thing you're not my girlfriend," Mary said.

"Yes, that's *one* thing we both agree on!" I exclaimed, and we both burst out laughing.

> *Change me Beloved into One who can honor, hear, and follow my inner guidance. May I trust You are guiding me in every moment. Let my mind shimmer with the radiance of positive thoughts. Grant me the courage and clarity to follow Your Divine nudges.*

27. *You Can't Stiff God*

My Virgo friend Alyx was busy juggling two careers: deep-tissue bodyworker and mystery writer. During one stretch, she was giving a huge number of massages to stressed-out folks and was beyond exhausted.

One morning she got a frantic call. A new client had strained her back and wanted an emergency slot. Alyx agreed to see her that Saturday morning rather than sleep in.

The session lasted a grueling and intense two hours; the woman, in severe pain, was demanding. At the end, she opened her wallet and said, "Damn, I forgot my checks! Where's the nearest ATM?"

Alyx gave her directions . . . and never saw her again.

Now, many people would be fuming and ranting after an experience like this. But fortunately Alyx was able to just let go.

She told me, "You know, I felt sad for the poor thing. After all I've been through, I finally trust that I'll always have enough. Most time when there's a loss, it's followed by a gain . . . if I'm open. But this lady kept moaning that she never got what she needed; her actions will likely just bring more of the same. I lit a candle for her."

Two days after that fateful massage, Alyx got a phone call.

Her recent manuscript had just been picked up by a major publisher.

> *Change me Divine Beloved into One who knows that you are my unlimited Source. May I neither fear loss nor cling to gain. Let me forgive anyone who has hurt me, knowing that You alone provide for me in the most surprising ways.*

28. Gifts at the Door

Someone was knocking at my apartment door. I asked who it was and heard an unfamiliar voice. Through the peephole appeared a rumpled-looking fellow. I asked him what he needed, without opening the door.

He said softly, "Oh, don't worry, you don't need to open it," and then began to shove the most gorgeous envelopes under the door, like a secret stash of love notes, each one a calligraphic wonder, ornately beribboned. I heard him make some shuffling noises, then go away.

Eventually, I opened the door to a *pile* of boxes filled with incredible gifts. I'm not much of a material girl, but everything was exactly my taste: cashmere shawls in every color, glittery purses, scented oils in cut-glass bottles.

I've often thought about this dream. What if it's about receiving the Gift of the Moment, even when it seems to come from an unappealing source? The Divine is aware of everything we need, even our most secret, hidden tastes. And for all I know, the gift-bearer was a scruffed-up saint, like Rumi and Hafiz, who have been said to visit those who love them in all kinds of disheveled disguises!

Change me Divine Beloved into One who can embrace the gift of each moment, even when it comes in a puzzling form. Let me accept whatever comes, like a secret present from God Herself.

29. *The Ticket Guru*

I once splurged on a great seat at a Queen concert because I hardly ever go to live music, and if I do, it's only to see people I'm wild about. So I was in the tenth row on the aisle, right next to the runway where Adam Lambert would spin all his flamboyantly fabulous gold-lamé-and-black-leather magic. I was sitting there, marveling at the shocking splendor of being so close, when this guy sat down next to me just as the show started.

He said he had just gotten his amazing seat for seventy-five dollars, which seemed almost impossible. But he looked for real so I asked how. He said, "I'll tell you. I've done this for hundreds of shows.

"I go to the box office just before it starts and ask if there's a last-minute stray ticket for under a hundred dollars that's up close. If there isn't one, I do the same thing with the scalpers. Since the event is about to begin, you wouldn't believe how often I get a ticket they couldn't sell for eight hundred dollars or more. They don't want to take a total loss. I ended up three rows from Cher that way. Prince also."

Then he smiled. "Here's the trick," he said. "When I walk up, I honestly never care if I get in or not. I just won't

71

take less than an amazing seat. And I figure if I'm meant to get in, I'll get something incredible . . . and if I'm not, hey, I'll go have a beer and have fun anyway. I couldn't care less. I decided a long time ago to be happy either way."

"Hey, I *know* that trick," I said, grinning. "I think I somehow ended up writing a freakin' book about somethin' like that."

He looked at me like I was nuts, and then the show began.

> *Change me Divine Beloved into One who is content in all conditions. May I take action as guided, yet fully surrender the outcomes, trusting the perfect route always occurs. Let me release grasping and fear, knowing You alone open the right doors.*

DIVINE RELATIONSHIPS

Change me Divine Beloved into One who easily releases whatever needs to go and happily welcomes whatever needs to come. Let me trust Your Divine Plan and timing in every way.

My Beloved, free me from attachment to any situations that do not serve my highest good and Your Divine Will. Whatever needs to come, let it come. Whatever needs to go, let it go. All of my needs are always met.

I am Yours.

You are mine.

We are One.

30. *Let the Artist Eat*

My friend Ricki has spent much of her life helping others. She's not only been a full-time caretaker for the disabled, she's always had a wide net of friends and relatives to assist.

Yet down deep she's one big shimmering, hyperfertile creative vortex. She's an irreverent artist and a true original. I remember one year she built an insane and intricate Elvis-basket for Easter filled with miniature guitars and peanut-butter-banana sandwiches. Another time she made a Nativity creche out of Play-Doh, packed with Hindu gods. And then there's "Johnny M," the debonair drag king she sometimes plays on stage.

Years ago I began carrying a notebook whenever we talked because so many inspired thoughts would fall like ripe fruit from her inventive mind. She's an aesthetic jack-of-all-trades where writing, cartooning, and calligraphy all bloom in profusion.

But she never made the time to pursue these things.

When an important relationship ended, Ricki hit rock bottom. She saw how her incessant attention to others made her ignore herself and her own needs.

She's finally prioritizing the artist's life that had sustained her even as a kid.

She said, "I'm coming out of a lifetime daze. My ship finally came in and I saw the precious cargo was *me*."

She refuses to deny her own creative hunger at the behest of others any more.

Change me Divine Beloved into One who honors my deepest creative passions and needs. Help me value the talents You have given, the known and unknown. May I always make time to fill and replenish myself in every way.

31. The Perfect Mate

Once a woman called me for advice. She'd taken an expensive course to attract "The Perfect Mate," and within a month she *had*. For a while, she was thrilled she'd spent the money and reeled in her "dream come true."

But eventually she became more and more terrified she'd lose this perfect partner. Obsessed even. If they went into a restaurant, she was scared he liked the waitress. If he talked for long to her best friend, she wondered if he might be attracted to her, too. She kept thinking, "Well, I sure manifested him, but how the hell do I *keep* him?"

Of course, her very fear and insecurity were beginning to chase him away.

By the time she called me she was really alarmed, "Oh, my God, I'm even starting to read those moronic articles on the internet like '10 Ways to Keep your Man.' What's happened to me? I don't know if I need an intervention or an exorcism!"

I laughed and told her that the piece of the puzzle she never learned in that workshop was "offering." Because if the ego creates something, yes indeed, it will almost always fear losing it. That's just what egos do.

But offering is a whole other story. I suggested she could

say, "*Dear God, you know my deepest needs. The right partner is already selected if it is Your will. But if not, please free me from this prison of longing! Let me feel whole and happy with OR without this.*" Then the raging desire could melt into a preference.

Ironically, by giving her current relationship to the Divine, she could finally relax and enjoy it. If it turned out he wasn't the right One, she needn't worry. Whoever *was* would come instead.

God had her covered.

> *Change me Divine Beloved into One who trusts that the perfect relationship always arrives on time. Let me feel worthy and deserving of love. Allow me to release all current relationships of every kind into Your waiting arms. May all desires melt into preferences.*

32. First Date

A letter I once received:

Dear Tosha,

I've often thought how you quote the Tao Te Ching saying, "The beginning contains the end." So I want to tell you this story.

I'm a gay man who spent three years in an unhappy relationship. Though there were sparks when we met, I heard a huge warning bell on our first date.

Yes, the guy was charming, gorgeous and so my "type." But at some point, he reached across the table with a dazzling smile and asked, "You don't mind, right?"

Then used my silk scarf to clean his grimy glasses.

Yes, he did.

Saddest of all, I didn't know how to say, "I mind!"

We slid into a stormy union that was more of the same.

Your writings finally gave me the courage to get out, remembering my own dignity.

I'd been saying for a while, "Change me Divine Beloved into One who knows my own value. Let me receive the Highest in every way, including a worthy partner if it be Your will."

Then last year I met someone new.

On our first date my iPhone was on the table. He glanced at it, offering, "Wow, your screen's so dirty! Can I help?"

He cleaned it and handed it back with such kindness and care, it was all I could do to keep from crying.

Yes, I too knew a heck of a sign when I saw one.

Love to you,

Randall

> *Change me Divine Beloved into One who knows my own worth. Let me feel entitled to speak my truth with love. May I know I deserve to be surrounded by those who value me.*

33. Drop the Baggage

My former girlfriend and I were on vacation in the Yucatán. On arriving, we decided to take a few hours to bike into town until our room was ready. When we returned, we saw that the rental car's trunk had been pried open right in the hotel's parking lot.

The suitcases were gone.

Now most people might think, "What awful luck, and on your birthday, too! You're on your first vacation in a year and your luggage is stolen. What a drag."

But here's where inviting in the Divine and becoming crazy-open to Reality As It Is becomes interesting. Yes, it was a shock, but was it truly bad luck? Or was it oddly good? I know this sounds nuts, but despite the shock of it all, the experience held a gift.

We both quickly decided it wouldn't ruin our trip, since we still had passports, money, and the clothes on our backs. We each felt blessed to be with someone who wasn't freaking out and not only that, we remembered why were together.

Before that, there were weeks of sparring as tensions rose to the surface between us. But the theft forced us to become a team again. Soon we were lying in a hammock on the deck, drinking margaritas, cuddling and cracking up. I joked that whoever had the karma of stealing those damn bags was fighting now with his partner.

Besides, my own suitcase had been packed with books about detachment, of all things: a well-worn copy of the *Tao Te Ching*, another called *The Stoic's Way to Joy*, a couple on faith and surrender.

It was as if God had declared, "Enough already, just *live* this. Take the leap and let go. Come on, I'll catch you." With nothing to read, I could only *be*.

When the bags vanished, a mysterious weight went too, and never returned.

> *Change me Divine Beloved into One who can be wildly open to Life as it comes. Let me release what wants to leave, and welcome what wants to come, trusting that my needs are always met. Help me live from full openness and trust.*

34. Debbie and Abe

In 2012, four months to the day after my mom's passing, my father, Abe, died at eighty-nine. When I went to Mom's funeral in July, I sensed Dad would go soon after. He swore he would *not* stay on this planet without her. Debby had been his angelic dynamo who handled everything with devotion and humor during their sixty-six years together.

For better or worse, they were inseparable.

So there I was in the odd role of being deeply relieved about a visitation from Death. My worst concern was that Dad would stay trapped on earth, lost and bereft without Mom. But his decline began as soon as she went. I burst into tears of relief when I heard the news.

He was a feisty Aries Pig and she a forthright Pisces Tiger, so boy did these two have their battles. Almost every day. But they were determined to be together, one way or another. They loved to go dancing (and were quite the team on the floor). I prayed that Mom got some serious rest in her four-month vacation in heaven, because they might well be up to their old tricks once Dad joined her.

Dad had often been hard on Mom despite his love for her; after she passed, he had deep and terrible regrets. He was obsessed with making it up to her, insisting constantly,

"When I see her again, I'm going to make amends in every way. I'll shower her with the adoration she deserved all along until the end of time."

I believe he will.

Now one more thing.

Many people have written me with good intentions saying they're sorry I'm an "orphan" now. But actually I'm not!

How could I be an orphan if the Divine is my parent? To me, God is my mother and father in a literal and specific way. No abstractions. That's who sent them in the first place. And That's who brings everything else each day.

Eternity brings the lover, friend, mate, parents, children, pets, *all* of it.

So I promise, if you build an intense relationship with the Beloved as your own center, you'll never feel abandoned again. By any seeming loss. There may be hurt, or even times of aching loneliness, but never abandonment.

I miss especially being able to laugh and talk with my beautiful, witty mom. That is true. But to be honest, I am hugely relieved she and Dad are released from their suffering.

I feel relieved every single day.

I already feel contacted by them through music, billboards, license plates, and other incessant signs. They're both nearby, though unseen.

Perhaps they're even still dancing together in the moonlight.

After the latest fight.

> *My Divine Beloved, allow me to know who*
> *I REALLY am . . . a form of the Divine*
> *encountering endless sacred forms of You in*
> *disguise. Take any fear of death, filling me with*
> *the knowledge that we are eternally One.*

35. The Goddess Who Purifies Passions

Once, wandering on Union Street in San Francisco, I saw an exquisite yogini sculpture in the doorway of a shop. She was sitting in full lotus pose and made of gleaming marble. I asked who She was.

The owner said a name I'd never heard before and added, "She's the One Who Purifies All Passions. But that doesn't mean blocking or stopping them. Just offering them to Her so you're not their slave."

I smiled, loving his description.

He then asked if I'd like to take her home, but at a mere thirty-two hundred dollars I declined. Then I thought how funny it all was. I mean, did anyone actually need a statue to purify passions? The spiritual marketplace is always presenting one more trinket for transformation, each more gorgeous than the next. But the Divine inside can actually do the job perfectly without a single prop.

That Goddess lives within.

And She's only waiting to be asked.

*Change me Divine Beloved into One who
offers all passions and longings to You,
allowing them to relax into preferences. Let
me feel whole, knowing all true needs will be
handled. You are my sublime Source for all.*

36. Much More than Nothing

A gal named Cassie wrote to say she feared leaving her exhausting, messy relationship. She thought "something was better than nothing," especially during the holidays.

"Au contraire, dear Cassie," I wrote, "because *you're* not nothing. If you leave, you'll still have *you*. That's plenty. And never underestimate the depletion that comes from falling down the energy abyss otherwise known as The Wrong Partner.

"Besides, belonging to the Divine means you can honor Your own sacred Self. Then you never have to beg for crumbs. The people that are right will always come . . . if you feel worthy.

"So, Cassie, you never need to talk yourself into something that feels wrong. Or disrespects you. Or makes you jump through hoops. You already *are* Love, you don't have to win it. And a timely 'no' now can make room for a much bigger 'yes' later.

"The Divinely selected relationship is already picked, and you'll be guided to it in the right time and way."

Why not make room?

Change me Divine Beloved into One who experiences my true worth in every moment. Let me know not only that I deserve love but that I AM Love. May I trust that my own sacred Self will always draw those of similar vibration.

37. The Mirror God

The other day I was waiting at the ferry terminal when I saw this guy with like sixty necklaces on, gazing at himself in a fuchsia hand mirror with great admiration. Yes, just another beautiful San Francisco day. I was thrilled and dubbed him "Lord Krishna."

When I asked if I could take his photo, he was happy. Then someone walked by in an Armani suit on the way to the Financial District and gave him the most disdainful grimace. "Jesus, when are they gonna finally clean up these damn streets?" the guy muttered under his breath.

I wondered how Lord Krishna would react. But he just guffawed and said, "Honey, you sho can't please everyone! And if you try, it gon' be VERY, very boring. Now you takin' that photo or not, girl?"

As I left I said, "Well, you know, the haters just usually hate themselves. It's not about you."

"Oh, yeh, you got THAT right!" he agreed. "And that's why they surely do need the blessings."

Then he went back to gazing fondly in his fuchsia mirror.

*Change me Beloved into One who can
easily and generously send blessings to all,
even those filled with negativity or fear.
May I shower the planet with love, knowing
there's an unlimited ocean within me.*

38. Dish Therapy

Being born with so many planets in Aquarius, there's not much I can hear that shocks me. Whether someone harbors a secret crush on his sister-in-law, comes out as transsexual in her Mormon family, or tells me his pet iguana wrote his latest novel, it's all in a day's work.

But a call I received once from Daly City really shook me up.

Pam started by saying how much she'd enjoyed my recordings on Divine Order and the mind.

She liked them so much she'd given them to her daughter, Deb, who was in the midst of an ugly divorce. "Well," she said, "Deb loved knowing about the power of sending thoughts and blessings. She figured, if the mind is so strong, why only send good? So she's been lighting a candle and sending hatred to her ex ten times a day because of you. She's been visualizing up a storm, imagining every possible horror raining down on him. She's got a whole new lease on life!"

I was speechless.

Pam gleefully went on, "So she wanted me to thank you. Her psychic 'work' is finally paying off; bad juju has come to this creep. A car ran a red light, hit him on Guerrero

Street, and cracked some ribs. Now he can barely breathe. And he's losing his house, too. Oh, and his cat got feline leukemia. Deb is overjoyed."

Well, this was all *so* wrong I was dumbfounded.

You see, I understand the need to release anger when someone's hurt or abused you. No need to put on a faux-spiritual happy-face; we've all seen enough fake smiles hiding rage or disappointment. But the solution is to release the emotions. Get therapy. Work out. Get it out of your poor bod.

Or use my personal favorite, "dish therapy." Buy a bunch of cheap plates from the Goodwill and smash them against a wall, screaming like a maniac. Repeat as needed. Breaking things feels great!

But sending direct mental energy to harm people is a whole other deal. Intentionally wishing them ill and rejoicing in their suffering can only boomerang back. That's serious black magic. It will return to you, if not in this life, then another.

And often the payback can be immediate, terrible, and swift.

Similarly, the more good you send out, even to those who have been hurtful, the more good returns. Luckily, the universe knows how to keep karmic ledgers without our help in the form of spells and vitriol.

Besides, if the Divine is your Source, no one can take anything from you that is meant for you. There's no loss in

God's world. It can return in a new, surprising way, more abundantly than before.

God can refill your cup at any time.

But not if you're busy filling it with poison.

> *Change me Divine Beloved into one who can*
> *easily access all emotions bottled within me.*
> *Let me feel, bless, and release anger, resentment,*
> *or bitterness. May I release any emotions*
> *that block happiness and contentment.*

DIVINE TRUST

Change me Divine Beloved into One who always trusts where You guide me.

May I always have faith in following Your lead.

Let me bless my life's unfolding in all the ways that are right for me.

May I always know all is occurring in Divine Order and every need is always met in the right time and way.

May I always trust You.

May I always know We are One.

39. The Lion Queen

Recently at one of my favorite hot springs, I overheard this story.

Amber had been living and hiking in the mountains near Calistoga forever, and knows the trails like the lines in her palm. Yet once, on a densely foggy Sunday, she got lost.

Because she'd only planned to walk briefly, Amber wore sandals and carried no water, food, or jacket. She quickly realized she was in trouble. After hours searching for the path, Amber gave up and spent the night in the soft needles under a pine tree, sleeping fitfully and freezing.

While she knew how to collect rainwater and forage for herbs, by the next afternoon her confidence was beginning to crumble. Search planes could be heard overhead, but no matter how much she waved and screamed, no one saw her in the fog.

As darkness fell on the second night, fear followed close behind.

The clincher came when she started to bleed. Then she spied a mountain lion watching from some nearby foliage. Everyone knew blood was prime bait; other attacks had happened in the area.

Initially, her panic was overwhelming. She shook with terror, her heart raced.

Then, her soul took over.

Amber lay in the dirt and prayed with her whole being, "If this is my time, so be it. I totally surrender. Just take me. I release completely to my destiny." A peace descended she had never before known. All resistance melted.

An hour later, the lion was gone. She suddenly remembered that as a Leo, the animal was her own totem.

From that point on, Amber was completely present and open, knowing she could survive one moment at a time. Staying in the now, she had no worry, no problem at all.

After three days she found her way, crawling, to the ironically named Dead Man's Road. Dehydrated, hungry, cold, and filthy, with two severely sprained ankles, Amber felt lucky to be alive.

And changed forever.

She told me, laughing, that the night before the hike her mom had called, pushing her to find "a husband who could save her." Amber had insisted that while an interesting boyfriend might be fun, she sure didn't need to be saved . . . *by anyone*.

While a rescue team of a hundred volunteers in Lake County had searched for seventy-two hours, indeed no one had found her.

Amber had to save *herself*.

With a big dose of cosmic assistance.

Change me Beloved into One who knows You are the ultimate protection. Let me stay fully in the moment, anchored in Divine strength. Fill me with courage and calm so I may endure even the hardest trials, trusting You will carry me. I am safe, I am Yours alone.

40. No Bag O' Bones

You never know who's longing to support you if you open yourself up to their help, either from this world or from other realms as well. In the last couple of months before my mother passed, she promised repeatedly she'd assist from the Other Side. In particular she wanted to allow my writing to get everywhere it was meant to go. She deeply believed in it.

I think of her now as my perfect Astral Manager.

Well, one day toward the end, Mom, Dad, and I were sitting in their kitchen, with my dad tearfully pledging he would visit Mom's grave with flowers. "Every single day," he solemnly vowed, "Debby, I swear, I won't miss a day!"

She rolled her eyes and gave him one of those playful but withering looks I had adored my whole life. "Really?" she asked, amused. "Well, don't BOTHER! Where do you think I'll be? Lying in the dirt like a cold bag of bones? Well, God and I have big plans together. Very big. So I'll be busy. And when you're ready, You can come help too!"

Dad looked shocked but Mom had it all perfectly figured out.

As usual.

Change me Divine Beloved into One who
understands the true meaning of Death.
Remove my fear of dying. Open my vision
to the Eternal. May all transitions lead me
into ever-deepening union with You.

41. The Karma Magnet

Karma is a funny thing. At twenty-one, fresh out of college, I never thought, "Wow, why not become a full-time psychic astrologer? What an efficient career move! In one fell swoop, I could be a marvelously wacky eccentric and disappoint my Jewish father, who prayed for a trial attorney."

But my accidental career took off when I enrolled in a six-week massage class. (That also went over well with my family, by the way. "Wait. You went to Yale to become . . . a deep-tissue masseuse? Are you kidding?")

Yet a hidden Divine plan was unfolding. While giving massages, I had spontaneous insights about my clients' lives and energy. I began to cautiously share what I was sensing. Eventually, during a session, a woman quietly asked, "Will you stop the massage and just talk with me? I need that more than anything."

She became one of my first readings.

I soon saw I didn't need touch for words to flow. Just being in people's presence, even on the phone, would bring insights into their lives. As I became obsessed with astrology and the tarot, the story unfolded even more. Yet I never went looking for this career; it just happened. (Good thing, since in India a career as a reader is considered a special destiny, not a choice. If you sought this work for money or power, horrible karma would follow.)

Well, the next thing I knew years had gone by. But at times when my schedule got slow, I dreamed of different work.

So when I saw an ad for interviews at a local design company I showed up. It seemed oddly alluring to sit in an office doing practical projects rather than flying around the ethers.

Soon I was called to meet my interviewer. As I walked in the door, the man behind the desk and I locked eyes intensely, then exploded into laughter.

Before me sat one of my favorite clients, Rob, who appeared often with one riveting dilemma or another.

"My God, will wonders never cease!" He slapped the desk in amazement. "Is this a joke? You don't think I'm gonna waste my precious time interviewing you. Why on earth are *you* here?"

"Well, things got slow and . . ."

"Hey," he said, grinning. "You know better. Don't worry if your calendar's open right now. You even told me in our last reading that God sometimes just gives us a rest."

Rob then proceeded to quote other eerily pertinent ideas I'd shared over the years.

I saw right then that he wore a tiny gold necklace of Lord Ganesh, the Hindu elephant god. I was sure even He was amused by all this.

Rob stood up abruptly, still laughing, "Now get the hell

out of here, sweetheart. I'm a busy guy. I gave you your reading and didn't even ask for a credit card. Go home and use the gifts God gave you. We need you."

He winked. "Call you next month."

> *Change me Divine Beloved into One who trusts Your timing in every way. Let me accept stretches of quiet and rest, knowing they recharge me for future action. May I trust that change always comes at the perfect time. I am Your very own.*

42. Vision Board Bar-B-Q

Sometimes I joke that one day I just up and burned all my vision boards in a frenzy of Divine devotion.

Here's why.

While it's true, to some extent, that we create the world through our thoughts and feelings, that's far too simplistic. There's a Sanskrit term "prarabdha karma": the lessons that someone came here to learn in a given life. It's the Divine agenda that a soul comes to master, far beyond what the ego could request or even imagine. That's why every longing is NOT meant to instantly come true, no matter how much someone fixates or what *The Secret* promised. Whoever wrote that country-western song "Thank Heavens for Unanswered Prayers" actually knew what they were talking about.

For example, when I was in my twenties I had a wildly intense desire to travel. I've written about this in *Outrageous Openness*. I kept an adventure file bursting with photos of Morocco, Japan, India, Bhutan, Bali—all the spots I longed to see.

Nonetheless, for the next thirty years I was almost always kept from traveling. So many trips were canceled it became funny. Yet this didn't occur because I did something wrong; I didn't feel unworthy. It's heartbreaking when people beat themselves up for wishes that don't come true.

My prarabdha karma simply had a whole other plan.

Eventually I surrendered and just let go. I sensed I'd spent many incarnations running like a lunatic all over the place; I had a true gypsy heart. But *this* life contained a much deeper lesson. However painfully, I had to learn how to rest in the Now . . .

Without going anywhere.

I'm sure in other lives I played hooky from this particular class. But the jig was up; in this life I had no choice. Yet over time, my wanderlust went from a passionate need to a calm preference. Now I can see that all this writing, teaching, and even spiritual life would never have occurred without a short and ruthless leash.

Once you begin to align with the Divine, you begin to get what your Soul, not the small self, wishes. You start to trust the process.

So many years later, I'm starting to take a big trip or two. And I truly love it, since I'm still the same adventurer I was as a teen. But I'm content now, with or without.

I guess you could say I'm no longer a slave . . . to my passport.

Change me Divine Beloved into One who can allow Love to lead my life. May I offer myself completely to the Highest so all may occur as needed. Grant me peace and contentment wherever I am. Use me for the greatest good.

43. Intermission

Back when I used to give readings, I noticed how often people booked sessions during a time I call "between the movies." Each chapter of life can be like a film. Everyone is the cast, our surroundings are the set, and we're the star. But, often at certain karmic junctures, one movie ends, and we wait impatiently for the next.

Sitting in the unknown.

Imagine you're in a double feature. The first movie has ended, and there's an intermission. You've gone to get popcorn, maybe a drink. You're in the dark, contemplating all you just saw. Nothing to do but wait for the next show.

And sometimes our intuition even reveals the coming attractions.

I gave a reading once to a woman in a marriage she'd long known was dead. She was mustering strength to tell her husband of twenty years that she needed to go.

For the past year, she had experienced extreme shortness of breath. No medical tests showed any physical obstruction. Yet she felt more and more often as if the air were being squeezed out of her lungs by her life.

At the same time she kept having flashes of herself in a sun-filled studio with shiny wood floors, on her own.

When she called me, she was paralyzed by indecision and fear, overwhelmed by how to begin again. We talked about calling Divine Order into her life.

I suggested a prayer like, *"Dear God, this entire partnership belongs to you now. If I am meant to stay, make it obvious. If I am meant to leave, open the way. Fill me with courage to take the right actions. Speak and act through me. Guide me to the new life that's already waiting."*

A few months later, I spoke to her again. She had in fact left her husband with unexpected ease. He even agreed the marriage had ended long before.

Her new movie had begun. She was actually living in that small, sunny apartment with polished wood floors that she had "seen." She could breathe again.

It was perched in a building above a store called Next Chapter.

Change me Divine Beloved into One who can offer all decisions to You, breathing and flowing with the unknown. May I trust during times of transition that the perfect actions will be shown. Grant me patience to allow events to line up as they need.

44. Oklezgo!

So much angst comes from forcing a decision too soon. Often people intuitively sense what's coming, but it's not yet time to act. They impatiently try to push the Flow before God's lined it all up.

But when the right time comes, it just organically happens.

I'd known for a while a new car was on the horizon. I figured I'd be guided to the right one at the right time.

Then, the day before my birthday, the dashboard on my old Prius died in a wild frenzy of excitement on Highway 101.

After I recovered from the thrill of driving LA to Berkeley in a rainstorm with neither speedometer nor gas gauge, I called the dealer. He said, "Perfect! Last month that part got covered by warranty. Come in and we'll give you a week's free rental."

So they loaned me a Prius-C which I'd test-driven the year before. I remembered that when I'd first hopped in with the sales gal, the jazz station was blasting Miles Davis's "Kind of Blue." I was entering a blissed-out saxophone swoon just as she apologized and changed the dial.

"No, NO!" I yelled, "It's A SIGN!"

She thought I was kooky, even for Berkeley.

It hadn't been time to buy back then, but my week with the rental sealed the deal. So that cosmically selected blue car became mine after all. On the day of purchase, I invited the Divine to take everything over, including the price-wrangling.

As I drove from the lot, a cute green Miata sports car cut in front of me with the license plate OKLEZGO.

And so . . . we did!

Change me Divine Beloved into One who
invites You into even the most mundane
decisions. Open me to this playful, joyous way
to live, following the signs as they are shown.
I am Yours, You are mine, we are One.

45. Never Too Late

Back when I still did astrology, I had a client in her seventies who was constantly being advised to just curl up at her "advanced" age and wait to die. But Emma still had tons of energy; her chart told a completely different story.

"I sure don't feel done," she told me. "In some ways I've barely begun. Isn't that incredible?"

"Did you know," I asked, gazing at her fifth house of creativity and love crammed with six planets, "that you're actually an artist?" Emma's cheeks were suddenly wet with tears as she looked down and nodded her head. "Yes, I knew when I was young. But I fear it might be too late for all that."

"Well, it ain't over till it's over," I crowed, suggesting she say the following prayer for a couple of months. What the hell. She had absolutely nothing to lose.

"My entire life is in Divine Order, outside of all imagined limits. Only the Divine Will is my guide. Let whatever dormant talents I have emerge for the good of all. Give me the courage to let whatever is within me flow. Make me ready. Remove any fear or resistance. Open the way."

I didn't hear from her for three years.

And then an email. Even though she'd painted in her twenties, she'd found a sculpting class soon after we met.

Eventually, she moved to Brooklyn to pursue what became a wildfire of ecstatic artistic devotion. To her amazement, her work was now in small galleries.

Then, a second miracle occurred.

At seventy four she'd also been told her romantic life was "of course" long over. But amazingly, she had met and fallen in love with another artist, a woman; she was now having her first happy relationship ever. Her life took unimaginable twists just by offering that packed little "fifth house" to the Divine.

Change me Divine Beloved into One who is freed from the illusion of time. Protect me from the toxic views this culture holds about age. Help me be open to a miracle of regeneration in every way. May I know I'm a dazzling and eternal soul, not a chronological number.

46. The Missing Teeth

Years ago, back when I still gave readings at my home, a German woman named Ora booked a session. She was stunning, inside and out, in a dramatic Leo way, with a wild mane of curly red hair that trailed after her like an inferno. When I looked in her piercing green eyes, I could see only kindness and purity.

And yet, and yet, she had come because she truly suffered. She'd grown up as the only child in an alcoholic home. Her dad swung from generous to violent in a heartbeat, and her mom ran ragged all day fending off his disasters. Though Ora had been in a twelve-step program for codependency, she was still haunted by a childhood event she could not shake. In a way, it symbolized her whole life; she was desperate for help.

Back when she was a teen, she'd gone out to dinner with her parents one night. Her dad had dentures and occasionally went without wearing them until he had to eat. When the main course arrived, he looked at his wife and beckoned for the teeth from her purse. She rummaged through it, then whispered weakly, "No, I don't have them. They must be in your pocket."

Ora's dad pounded his fist on the table so the water glasses shook, and other diners looked over. "No!" he growled, "I gave them to *you*. You must have accidentally left them on the plate when the waiter took our appetizers."

Now this was an insane statement that made zero sense, but Ora's mom knew better than to argue. She sighed with deep resignation, "So *what* should I do?"

He shot her a disdainful look, then signaled the waiter with one finger. "Young man, my stupid wife has lost something important in your trash so she must look through all the bins in your kitchen. I need you to take her there *now*." Ora's mom sat looking exhausted and mortified.

The waiter seemed surprised by this nutty request but then just acquiesced. Something commanding about Ora's dad made people often obey him.

So Ora's mom was brought back to the kitchen to rifle through can after can of garbage, on a delightful denture hunt. Ora sat slumped at the table, her head in her hands, quietly crying. Her father fumed beside her in sullen fury.

A half-hour later her mom returned, empty-handed, pale, and wan. Nada. She'd emptied and examined every filthy trash can she could find. Her tired eyes glanced fearfully at her husband's reddening face. He truly was about to explode; sweat covered his brow. He reached for the handkerchief in his breast pocket.

And there they were.

The Teeth.

"Ohhhh, look!" he suddenly sang out. "They were here all along. Too bad you had to go through all that. What a *shame*."

In our work together, Ora saw how she'd replayed her mom's codependent drama in countless ways. She was constantly attracting the garbage of others, an unconscious yet devoted recruit in scavenger hunts commanded by crazy people.

She was ready to resign from being the world's best trash collector.

The Divine could finally bring a new life.

Change me Divine Beloved into One who feels deserving to set boundaries anywhere they're needed. Fill me with clarity and courage when I'm around those who are raging and destructive. May I always remember who I really am, a spark of Your Love, deserving of dignity, kindness, and self-respect. Keep me centered in even the most challenging situations, able to say no to abuse. Let me love myself as You love me.

47. The Only Intention

Occasionally someone tells me that the Universe won't know what to bring if I don't have a clear intention. But that's ridiculous if you think about it. The Divine is the Intelligence living in every cell of your body who actually created you *as* you.

Besides, I *do* have one single, overriding intention that's simply trumped all of the others.

It's available to anyone and is actually the strongest intention you could *ever* have:

Thy Will be done through me.

Use me. Take Me. Do what You will. Make me Your own.

And believe me, God knows what to do with *that* intention.

I don't think She gets confused at all.

> *Divine Beloved, change me into One who wants what You want. Let me trust that if I invite Your vast intelligence to guide me, all will unfold in wonderfully unimaginable ways.*

48. Get His Coat!

I once heard a story about Maya Angelou. She was throwing a party at her house and a guy started to loudly tell a story with horrible jokes about both black and gay people. Maya supposedly just yelled from the other side of the room, "Get that man's coat! Show him out of my house!"

The room went into stunned silence; some people were shocked. But she explained, "This is my HOME. You can't come into my home and say this. Say it in your own place if you like." And he was shown out.

Well, lately I've been thinking how our Beings are our homes as well. Yet we'll listen to all *kinds* of junk and absorb it like strong poison.

A woman named Jane told me yesterday that she was about to take a trip to Mexico for the first time. Everything was lining up like magic for her to go. She was hugely excited . . . until a "friend" began to fill her mind with terror. By the end, she'd convinced Jane that the minute she got off the plane in Guadalajara she'd probably be raped or mugged, if she wasn't shot first.

"But I guess," her friend ruefully chuckled, "if it's your time, it's your TIME. Ooh, honey, I'm so, sooo sorry you're not going somewhere safe and pretty like I did when I went to Hawaii. Anyway, I'd want you to tell ME if I was going so I'm just saying it from loooove."

Jane not only went into total anxiety, she also psychically felt . . . well, slimed. You can just feel it, right?

Luckily she did some research and realized that the violence was happening in Mexican border towns, and that things were quite different where she was going. People travel safely all the time to that beautiful country. The dark predictions came more from the other woman's fear, ignorance, and even jealousy than from any reality. Yet Jane *still* couldn't shake the anxiety that sullied her mind. She felt her trip had been ruined.

I suggested she get a coconut (like I do in *Outrageous Openness*) and mentally put all the negative energy into it. Release all her friend's darkness and then go smash the heck out of that thing. Let it all go and throw it out. (This ancient ritual from India was not to harm her friend in any way but to release the grip that her negative thoughts had on Jane's mind.)

She needed to not only purge her friend's energy but offer the trip to God, so I gave her this prayer:

"I now offer this entire trip to You. Guide me where You will, knowing I'm surrounded always by Your protection. Free me from those who even unconsciously might wish me harm. I am fulfilled and safe, held in the arms of Your Love."

Change me Beloved into One who is protected from all negative energy and predictions! Fill me with Your dazzling and radiant Light; make me a vessel for Your Love. I now release all fears I've absorbed from others! Let me trust ALWAYS where my own intuition takes me.

DIVINE FAITH

Divine Beloved, change me into One who lets You protect and guide me in every moment. Fill me with Faith, even in the most trying of circumstances.

May I always know Your radiant protection is present in every moment.

I am Yours.

You are mine.

We are One.

All is well.

49. *Just Like Madonna*

Once when I was sixteen, I had a memorable conversation with my aunt at Thanksgiving dinner. It all started when she asked how I was doing.

"Totally miserable," I mumbled, annoyed that she had broken my angst-filled reverie.

I then received a long, passionate lecture about how these were the best years of my life, and how it would all become worse, much worse, soon enough. I better embrace my youth while I could!

"Your nature is your nature, my darling," she concluded, while patting her lacquered brown beehive. "People simply can't change. If you hate yourself now, I promise you also will when you're forty. Even more so!" She lit one more Marlboro and inhaled. "I mean, look at *me*."

Though some part of me longed to rush to the bathroom, down a bottle of Tylenol, and save myself a lot of trouble, another part knew she was misguided. Completely.

Perhaps the ensuing years were my soul's response to that one Thanksgiving pep talk.

Somehow I always knew that life gives endless new beginnings, endless chances to remember who you *really are*.

Every seven years the cells in the body renew completely. Every twenty-one days, new thought patterns are encoded. Doesn't this mean we all can endlessly reinvent ourselves? Just like Madonna?

To prove my aunt wrong, I had to learn to be more self-accepting and elicit Divine help. Believe me, if I could invite these changes into my life, anyone can.

> *Change me Divine Beloved into One who knows we can evolve and open at any age. Let me welcome change in uplifting and surprising ways. Allow me to trust the process, diving ever deeper into Your love.*

50. The Praying Bunny

After yoga one day, I somehow slipped and tweaked my ankle. It was such a small event, I hardly noticed any pain at all, and just went on with my day.

Suddenly five hours later, in the middle of Haight Street, I could NOT walk. The foot refused to take any weight and began to throb.

Well, the good thing about focusing on Divine Order is prayers kick in of their own volition. They just arise. "Show me what you wish, show me what to do," I began. "The perfect actions are already picked . . . guide me . . . please open the way!"

You don't waste any time blaming yourself or resisting. You just start praying your tail off.

I really couldn't walk. A sudden impulse came to call my acupuncturist, though he keeps limited hours, rarely answers his phone, and never has immediate slots. But this time . . . he *did*. I had no idea how I'd even get there.

It took twenty minutes to hop back to the car. I must have looked like a wacky, intensely praying bunny rabbit left over from Easter.

Then, lo and behold, a parking space opened *right* in front of the office, which had never happened before. An hour of needles, massage, and Arnica healed the worst of my pain.

I walked out.

Who knows what would have happened without aligning with the Divine?

This stuff is just so damn practical.

Change me Divine Beloved into One who remembers to call on You in emergencies, knowing nothing is too big or small. Help me relax as You guide the way, even during injury or illness. I'm always safe in Your care.

51. Zen of Parking Lot

7:50 a.m. Core Power Yoga Lot, Berkeley.

I'm in my Prius finishing up a phone call before class. Suddenly a large black SUV whisks into the space next to me, so achingly close I can no longer open my door.

I roll down my window, giggling.

"You're kidding, right?" I say to the girl, pointing at the almost empty lot. "I mean, really? Why here? Why me? Did ya just want to get to know me better?"

She looks at me blankly, shrugs her shoulders, gets out of the car, and strolls upstairs.

7:52 a.m. Wow. Wedged behind wheel, momentarily fuming.

7:53 a.m. Wondering: Do I want to be mad and waste the morning with this? Does my body need the assault of even momentary resentment while on the way to yoga of all places?

Or . . . do I want to feel compassion, plus a dose of good-humored astonishment, by just rolling with it all?

7:54 a.m. I spend a full minute contemplating how to

twist myself like a true yogini over the gear shift to slither out the other door. But then, I have the Life-Changing Realization: I can MOVE THE CAR.

7:55 a.m. I move.

Change me Divine Beloved into One who can flow in the moment, finding humor and acceptance in even the silliest events. May I accept Reality as it is. Free me from the prison of duality, knowing all I encounter is my own Self. Let me adapt to what I cannot change, seeing gifts in every dilemma.

52. *Waiting for Change*

A dream.

I was living in a beautiful desert that had only one tiny post office with no other shops nearby. My entire car was filled to the brim with packages to mail. Some were books, others were lovely wrapped gifts. A sign said CASH ONLY.

Somehow I had a hundred-dollar bill in my wallet but the post lady said, "Oh, I can't break this right now!" She turned to the people in line. "Does anyone here have change?" No one did.

I was so eager to mail these, I asked if she could keep the difference and give it to me later. She peered at me curiously, then shouted, "Lady, what do you think this is? A tab at the local bar? *We're the post office!* We don't do that! You'll just have to wait until the right change arrives."

Sometimes, no matter what you're longing to share with the world, you just have to let the Universe become ready. Then everything arrives on its own time.

*Change me Divine Beloved into One who truly lets
You take the lead. Fill me with patience and faith
as you line up all pieces of the puzzle. Let me trust
the right changes always come at the right time.*

53. Dive In

Sometimes I get letters like, "I went to Catholic school and I'm terrified of praying 'wrong.' I don't want to make a mistake."

But listen. If you invite the Divine fully into your life as Love, you don't have to worry about that. God just wants to be included! You'll pray however you're drawn and eventually, the Divine will become your closest Beloved, a Presence endlessly speaking through your own intuition. Your whole life becomes a communion with this Force.

What matters is the constant invitation, and the remembering.

So I always figure, invite the Divine, see yourself as One with that Love, and forget the rest. *This is your Beloved.* Open your heart, offer everything, and you can't go wrong. If you fell in love with someone, you wouldn't fear every minute that you'd say the wrong thing.

Years ago I found this little green tome called *The Abundance Book*. Its main message was simple and fabulous: God is the Giver of All. Period, the end. Just know God as Giver and you'll understand Divine Source. You'll welcome all the ways the Divine might wish to give.

When I read this, my world turned upside down. I suddenly saw how often I blocked what wished to come by dictating how it *needed* to come. I'd confused each individual rivulet with the ocean of Divine Abundance itself.

But here's the funny thing. The author kept warning over and over, "You *must* do this for forty days! If you don't the Plan won't work!"

Well, you know me. I found his rigidity so annoying I just had to stop on day twenty. On *principle*.

But truth be told, my life and finances still changed completely. What mattered was knowing that God was the Source . . . and being ridiculously open to receive.

Depending on your readiness, you could get that understanding in one minute or forty days. Even right now.

Because someone pointed out to me once that the letters in Divine also spell Dive-in.

Maybe that's all God's waiting for?

> *Change me Beloved into One who allows the*
> *Universe to give to me every way It chooses.*
> *May I be fully open to receive, knowing the*
> *Divine is my complete Source. Let me release*
> *all perfectionism and fear of "doing it wrong."*
> *Let me dive straight into Your heart O God.*

54. Personal Service

At the end of my first trip to New York City in seven years, I arrived at Penn Station to catch my train to the airport. I'd always found the complete chaos of that place overwhelming in the past. Not exactly ADHD friendly. They announce the track for each arriving train at the very last moment, then people dash like frantic lemmings to catch it before it goes.

I could feel my heart panicking, so I began to call in the Divine for help.

Out of nowhere, this attendant walks up, staring at my neck. He's noticing all my tiny deity medallions: Lakshmi, Ganesh, Jesus, Guadalupe, a Mayan medallion from Mexico, a Hamsa for my inner Jew. Yep, there's a real crowd there.

But he only cares about my little ornate Russian cross of Jesus. He asks, "Hey, you a Catholic?"

I say, "No, but I sure do love Him madly along with all the others . . ."

He rolls his eyes like he's thinking, "Oh my freakin' god, *another* crazy yoga person." But suddenly he exclaims, "Okay then, dat's good enough for me!" and takes me all the way through the ticket line and straight onto the train.

Don'tcha think Jesus must have told him to help?

Change me Divine Beloved into One who remembers to call on You in even the most confusing situations, large or small. May I lean on Your strength, knowing Your grace can unravel any dilemma. Let me honor my own unique relationship to You, allowing it to express itself in whatever way most deeply fits my own heart.
I am Yours. You are mine. We are One. All is well.

55. Unholy Scam

The Divine made You as a holy expression of Love exactly as You are.

But many get told they need to *become* worthy of love from other humans, and even from God.

However, trees, grass, seashells, kittens, dragon lizards, spider monkeys, Pomeranians, chipmunks, and just about anyone and anything besides deluded, brainwashed humans do NOT feel this way.

Sense a scam?

Here's the Truth. You already *are* Love.

And You already *are* Worthy.

This is a central tenet of existence, independent of age, race, gender, charisma, height, weight, bank account, sexual orientation, and genital size.

Over time, the Divine can reveal this, if it is sincerely offered.

Why the heck *not?*

Change me Divine Beloved into One who knows without question my own beauty, worthiness, and desirability. Let me remember constantly who I am, a spark of Divinity, of Love, in a temporary human form. Awaken me from any traces of amnesia; may I always recall my true nature as radiant Light.

56. Heavenly Messengers

When *Outrageous Openness* first came out, I took the book to a metaphysical bookstore in Oakland. The owner glanced at the Table of Contents, then wrinkled her nose as if I had brought in a hunk of stinky cheese. She declined it, saying, "Well, what *is* this? Is it spiritual? New Age? Humor? You'll never sell it. And with so many books competing, well, I hate to tell ya but this one is doomed."

Thank God I knew to not absorb her prediction. While I don't think she meant ill, she only knew how to view these matters from a "scarcity lens."

"But I don't even believe in competition," I answered calmly. "It'll just go wherever it's needed most. I know this sounds mad, but eventually anyone on the planet who might need it, will have it. It's been offered to the Divine, so I only walk through the doors that open."

Suddenly the door of the store did indeed fly open and a striking man and woman strode up. The guy was about seven feet tall and looked like a charismatic cross between Will Smith and Jesus. The woman had a blonde Afro like a celestial halo and barely came to his elbow. He spied the book in my hands.

"Oh, my God," he yelled, "What IS that!? Wow, love the title. Do you have more? I need one NOW!"

We all went outside to do the deal, laughing as traffic whizzed by on Telegraph Avenue. As he pulled bills from his wallet, the woman began to sing in an unearthly voice, as if she were channeling from an otherworldly gospel choir. "God will bless this book," she proclaimed, hand in the air, eyes half-closed, head flung back. "God will bless this book! Don't you worry, I'm here to testify. All your trouble will be worth it. It is done!"

I had gone through such trials with the production of OO that I burst out crying. Then we all hugged and they left with their copy.

To this day I wonder if they actually were angels from above.

Change me Divine Beloved into One who can trust that You alone are the Source for all. Free me from the illusion of scarcity and competition. Let me trust that all who need what I have to offer always find me and that all needs are always richly met. I am Yours alone.

57. Rock the Choir

If the Universe wants you do to something, don't worry. It'll either give you the ability or send the help . . . if you are open.

Once I had a dream.

Someone asked me to conduct a big choir. That was just insane because though music is an obsession of mine, I can't even carry a tune. So I just stood there, frozen, praying like mad to be shown what to do.

At that moment, a dear friend who's a violinist came over and whispered, "Got this one sooo covered, babe."

She started happily conducting, totally in her element: impossible for me, effortless for her.

Such a huge relief for this Capricorn who grew up with a sign over my bed saying, *"If you don't do it, it won't get done."*

Learning how to receive Divine help shifts everything.

One of the happiest dreams ever.

Change me Divine Beloved into One who gratefully receives all help You send. Let me release the old and useless idea that I must carry the burden alone. Let me trust you always send the right assistance. May I feel worthy and accept!

58. Decisions in Thirty Seconds or Less

Here's the truth: I actually have *no* idea how to live like a "normal" person. That experiment was a complete, unmitigated nightmare.

So here's an example:

I once had a week to decide whether to go forward with a surgery. I was bombarded with differing opinions from doctors, friends, the internet, all of it. (Once you get on the web with this stuff, you could go crazy.) At the peak of confusion, I luckily remembered that I wished it all to belong to God, not the small self. Everyone's opinions were secondary.

Besides, with all the fire in my chart, some passionate, impulsive choices in the past had gotten me in a *lot* of trouble! I've often thought a helluva comedy book could be called *Well, It Seemed Like a Good Idea at the Time.*

Now I only wish for Divine Will.

So here's what I do with any big choice, praying intensely to the Highest, clearest, most intuitive part. Anyone can do this:

"Dear Divine, This All belongs to You. If I'm headed

the wrong way, please please STOP me now. Block me if I'm making a mistake. And if I am meant to do this, I offer all to You. Bring me dynamic clarity and courage as You open the way. I am entirely Yours."

For me, that's the only way to get ANY freakin' peace, and yes, it works like a charm.

So, with help like this, remind me again why anyone would want to be normal?

Change me Beloved into One who can offer all major decisions to You. Let me trust You're always guiding me through my intuition in the right directions. May I always remember that if something is meant to be, "Out of no way God finds a way."

59. But You Can't Miss the Boat if You Are It

About fifteen years ago I was excited to be going to San Miguel de Allende in Mexico with a pal. When we arrived, we piled into a shared cab for the ride to town.

An American looked at us and said, "First trip? Ohh, so sad you're coming now. I mean, it's been ruined. You *should* have been here ten years ago. *That's* when it was incredible. Too late."

Then she proceeded to tell us for the next five minutes all the ways we'd missed our chance to experience heaven. The traffic, noise, tourists, elevated prices, on and on.

Finally I'd *had* it. I looked at her as kindly as I could muster and said, "Hey, we're here *now*. We weren't *meant* to be here then. Now is our time. And we want to be open to it as it is right Now. Could you freakin' stop?"

So she did. And yes, it was absolutely amazing.

So many people are taught to fear they may have missed the boat in one way or another. But here's the truth. Whenever you get to wherever you are, *that's* your time. You can't be late to your Destiny. And if you embrace that, if you're outrageously open to life as it presents itself (or you pray to be), this is such a beautiful way to live.

Plus so much easier!

> *Change me Divine Beloved into One who can embrace the moment exactly as it is, knowing everything happens for the Highest way when I am open. May I lavishly bless it All and be a conduit for your Love. Let me trust every true need is always, always met. I am Yours. You are Mine. We are One. All is well.*

60. The Botulism Workshop

Years ago someone handed me a free ticket to a workshop that changed my life in an unexpected way. I found the title "Make My Dreams Come True . . . and I Mean NOW" so odd, I had to go.

It was taught by a *New York Times* best-selling author who shared tricks for attracting your desires. There were colorful posters on the walls with slogans like "You Deserve It ALL" and "Get Everything, You're Worth It." During the breaks, the seventies disco classic "More, More, More" blasted over the loudspeakers.

He told us he was a "master manifester" and taught seminars in every country. He also shared an estate near a golf course with his beautiful, blonde wife. But to me none of that mattered. It was his heartfelt, surprising confession just before lunch that shook my entire world to the ground.

He admitted that though his book was currently number four on the "List," he was deeply disappointed. Why wasn't it number *one*? This really tortured him. He genuinely begged us to visualize it triumphant at the top, trouncing all the others for a long, long time. Then and only then he could have some peace.

But I only saw one thing: He had fulfilled so many desires and *still* wasn't happy.

Now don't get me wrong, I wasn't judging him. In a funny way, I admired his candor. I honestly felt compassion since, under the flash and glamour, he was clearly suffering.

His admission hit me like a splash of ice-cold water on a scorching day. I woke up. Suddenly I knew: No matter what manifesting creates, it can never bring peace or contentment. Lifetime after lifetime it will never, ever be enough.

The insatiable ego *always* longs for more. No matter *what* it gets.

Aptly, my partner and I both got food poisoning at lunch that day and spent the rest of the workshop puking in our room. We joked weakly that spiritual nausea had finally caught up with us.

Two days later, I emerged, shaky but transformed. I could finally see how chasing wishes, as seductive and sometimes effective as it could be, was like leaping head-first down an endless rabbit hole.

Actually that workshop propelled me directly into the waiting arms of the Divine. I began to passionately invite a Higher plan to truly take over and guide my life.

If I knew then what I know now I would have told that poor guy, "Listen, if you *offer* your book to the Divine, you won't have to worry if you're even *on* that damn list. Those who are meant to find your work, *will*. It'll go everywhere it needs to and you'll be shown the right actions at the right time. Everything that's meant to happen will . . . plus you'll actually be free to relish it."

Anyone can learn this.

Change me Divine Beloved into One who offers all desires to You to do with as You wish. Let me cast off the burden of longing. May I trust that whatever is meant to happen, will always happen. Let me serve You, first and foremost, in every way.

DIVINE SURRENDER

Take me over and do what You will.

    I am Yours alone.
    Just take me over and do what You will.
    Make me Yours.
    You are Mine.
    We are One.
    All is well.

61. *Leaving the Ring of Fire*

While the popular Law of Attraction holds a measure of truth (we attract according to our vibration), I find it more simplistic than the way karmas actually unfold.

So here's a spiritual progression I've watched over the years:

Stage 1: You feel depressed and powerless from a culture that teaches fear, shame, and self-reproach.

Stage 2: You become excited discovering this law and make heartfelt lists of all your burning desires. "How wonderful life will be once this all comes true!"

Stage 3: The tendency to "try to manifest" becomes all-consuming. Some wishes hatch while others do not as Laws of Karma coexist with the Law of Attraction. Not all options are actually open at any given moment.

A crossroads is reached. Realizing that this world is more than a wish-fulfilling tree, you may become bitter or despairing. "I worked sooo hard trying to get this and it STILL didn't happen!"

But if you are sufficiently exhausted or desperate:

Enter Stage 4: An intense longing arises to invite the Divine. Weary of chasing and suffering, you radically crack open to another way. This is a profound and holy moment.

Stage 5: You begin to see that holding a high vibration aligned with the Divine lets everything happen in a spontaneous way. "Trying to manifest" feels like an unnecessary burden. Desires are offered to the Highest, rather than clutched. A sense of peace and contentment grows.

Stage 6: Alignment with the Divine slowly deepens. Miracles accelerate. Everything begins to happen through you rather than by you. Trust increases that the Universe actually knows what It's doing, has your back, and loves you madly.

Stage 7: You discover that some of those strongest desires actually *were* the Divine Plan after all. Surprise, surprise. (And the ones that weren't are no longer wished for anyway.)

God just wanted you to relax, surrender, and receive.

Optional but Lucky Stage 8: You fall madly in love with the Divine and begin to want *only* what It wants.

Change me Divine Beloved into One who can rest in Your arms. Let me offer my deepest desires to You to be shown Your Will. Drench me in Your love, make me Your servant, guide my way.

62. The Amnesiac Garden

When all actions are offered 100 percent to the Tao from the depth of your heart, everything unfolds according to Divine Order in the right time and way. You needn't have anxiety. The deepest needs of your heart are known.

This morning a friend told me her huge, gorgeous garden was covered in unexpected frost when she woke up. She immediately thought, "Oh, man, all those months of hard, hard work. All lost!"

She immediately offered all the vegetables and plants to the Divine and said, "Okay, whatever! Whatever is meant to be, will be. I surrender." As she brought the food inside she realized most plants had survived the frost just fine. And whatever did not, was not "hers" anyway to worry about.

Then she said to me, laughing, "I just got total spiritual amnesia and forgot for a minute Who all that lovely lettuce and zucchini belonged to in the first place!"

Change me Divine Beloved into One who offers ALL to You knowing everything occurs in the right time and way. Release me from all fears of loss or attachment to gain. Let all come and go as You wish, knowing that You alone are the Source of all true abundance. I am Yours. You are Mine. All is well. We are One.

63. The Perfect Phlebotomist

Recently I had to go for a routine blood test, something I avoid like the plague. I have teensy veins, like a child's, and the last time I got one, the nurse went at me like a human pincushion. I had bruises for days. No one's *ever* found a vein on the first try so they've always terrified me.

This time I knew to completely offer myself over to the Divine. *"Dear Beloved, my body is Yours alone. I give this test to You; guide me to the right clinic where the perfect technician is already waiting. Take me in your arms and guide me, I am entirely Yours."*

I ended up on a whim at a lab in Oakland and amazingly, the waiting room was almost empty. An adorable, friendly guy with five diamond stud earrings and a hoodie poking out from his lab coat greeted me from behind the counter.

"Hey, you picked the right day!" he said. The receptionist filled out my paperwork from my insurance card while he took me straight back into the lab. Did I mention that he looked like he was maybe nineteen and played in a hip-hop band during lunch? I spied a skateboard in the corner.

For a second, my mind flared in fear, wondering how

much experience he actually *had*. But my body knew better. I had turned it over completely and this was where I had ended up.

I suddenly sensed this dude was gonna be *genius* at this. When I sat down, he told me to make a fist, then smiled as he looked me in the eye. He tied my arm and simply said, "Chill, mama."

That made me laugh. He found a vein on the first try. In and out of that lab in no time; a total miracle. I wanted to hug him . . . and so I did.

Offer, offer, offer . . . even this stuff. You never know who God might send.

*Change me Beloved into One who can offer
my body entirely to You. Let me give every
feared test or procedure over to You completely.
Allow me to fully relax and be carried in
Your arms, trusting the Divine outcome.*

64. Shattered Glass

About ten years ago, I parked in Japantown in San Francisco. At the time I was still having trouble limiting my work schedule. (Find me, please, a Capricorn Sun, Moon, or Rising who sometimes doesn't have this problem.) When I didn't pay attention, I overbooked myself with nonstop work, and seriously suffered later.

I went inside to get a quick bowl of soba noodles. When I returned a half-hour later I saw glass all over the sidewalk. Someone had smashed my window.

But they took only one thing: my appointment book.

CDs, change, even a leather jacket in the backseat were all untouched. At that moment, a spontaneous rain shower began.

While I sat there in mild shock, an older, distinguished-looking man walked up smiling and asked if I was okay. When I said yes, he slowly opened his wallet, then threw a twenty-dollar bill on the seat. "Just in case you need," he said over his shoulder as he ambled away.

I drove across the Bay Bridge, soaked and exhilarated, blasting Nina Hagen while rain poured in through the broken window.

While I had a complete mess trying to reschedule every-one's sessions with me, I rebooked it all . . . leaving far more space for rest and play this time.

I had learned my lesson.

> *Change me Divine Beloved into One who*
> *can fully offer my schedule to You, so my*
> *life can be in balance. Let me take rest*
> *whenever necessary, trusting that one way*
> *or another all needs will always be met.*

65. I'm Right Here

Some days I still really miss my mom, Debby, who left this planet in 2012. Yet I honestly don't believe in death in the conventional way. To me, our souls continue eternally even though a particular body drops away, and we eventually prepare for another life to learn more lessons if needed.

In fact, the people we love who have passed on are often intensely trying to help us, sometimes even with frustration as we ignore them. While I do sense Mom's presence often, the loss of that particular form still sometimes swamps me. It's only natural.

Mom's number in my iPhone constantly tortured me for a year after her death. One day I just couldn't take it anymore so I pressed delete.

Then I started to cry in my car at a red light with my windows down. A black Honda Civic pulled up, driven by a woman in her thirties with an elegant blonde French twist just like Mom's back in the day. "Okay," I thought, smiling through my tears, "nice move. You've definitely got my attention."

Suddenly the woman began joking loudly with her little son in the seat next to her. "What the heck are you crying for? I'M RIGHT HERE!" She shook her finger at the boy playfully. "What is *wrong* with you? Can't you see me?"

Her mix of exasperation, love, and humor was so similar to Mom's that I burst out laughing. How on earth could I doubt her tangible presence?

> *Change me Divine Beloved into One who knows the true nature of our souls. Awaken me to the knowledge of the Eternal. Open me to all messages, signs, and love from those who have passed on, trusting that death is yet one more dimension. We are One.*

66. The Sacred Meal

When a particularly intense desire has been cooked in the fires of offering and detachment, it eventually transmutes into a preference.

And sometimes the process is painful as hell. Because lifetimes of attachments, delusions, and addictions are being stripped away and transformed.

But eventually, if the offering is sincere, you become free of this bondage. You just let go.

Detachment has come.

In Sanskrit this is called vairagya.

You're no longer a Total Deranged Addict.

You're finally whole in your own skin, with *or* without.

You're okay either way.

You might *prefer* it, but you're no longer broken inside.

Ironically, that's often when the preference can finally be received and enjoyed as a sacred meal.

It's as if God sits you down, whisks out a perfect white tablecloth with a flourish, then serves you and says, *"Bon appétit!"*

Change me Divine Beloved into One who offers you my deepest longings, trusting You know exactly how to handle them. Lead the way completely; free me from my chains. And please let me know my wholeness and freedom most of all.

67. Soda Pop

Donna, a fiery life coach with four planets in Aries, wrote me once to say, "Your approach to life feels awfully passive. I dream up everything I want so I can manifest my next big batch of desires. I don't sit there twiddling my thumbs."

Here's what I wrote back.

Look, that's one way to live. But believe me, you're not just lying around if you offer yourself to the Divine. It's a shift from indulging the small self to serving the Great One. If your inner conviction is "Let my highest Destiny unfold," or "May I be a conduit for Good," your life can't help but change.

Surprising and even inconceivable events hatch of their own volition.

And sometimes, once they line up, you barely have time to think straight. The Divine is literally *using* you day and night in the most oddly fulfilling ways because It knows you inside out. Your talents, passions, longings. I mean, who made you anyway?

And if you say, "Great, take all of me! Let me serve a Divine Plan," the Universe definitely responds. It sure won't ignore that plea.

Your whole vibration elevates to a different dimension.

Sort of like drinking clear water from an alpine stream rather than a fizzy bottle of Diet Coke.

After all, at some point in the evolutionary road, soda goes flat . . . and your soul does get really, really thirsty.

> *Change me Divine Beloved into One who offers myself to You. Fill me with faith and trust that You know my deepest needs and longings. Use me for the highest good. I am Yours, You are mine. We are One. All is well.*

68. The Lost Box

A friend sent me expensive herbs by overnight mail so they'd remain fresh. Though I received a notice that the package had arrived at my building, no one could find it. So I went to the post office to search.

Nada.

The next day I tried back again, waiting in a line into infinity to talk to someone. Again, nothing. Finally, on the third voyage into the void, otherwise known as the U.S.-Postal-Service-after-budget-cuts, I remembered the Truth: nothing need ever be chased.

What's meant for you will always come.

"Go *home*," I heard inside. "Let it come to *you*. After all, it's the Divine's, not yours. If you need it, it'll come. If not, let it go. God's the One who sent the herbs and God will deliver . . . or not."

I let go.

As I drove up to my building, the mailman literally chased me into the garage, yelling, "Good lord, where on earth have you *been*? I've searched for you everywhere."

He smiled, waving the lost package.

Sometimes you just have to stop and do nothing but receive, receive, receive.

Change me Divine Beloved into One who lets go easily and stops chasing outcomes. Let me offer all my needs to You, knowing You bring sacred solutions at the right time. May You guide my way in every moment, showing the perfect actions. Let me feel worthy to open and receive in every way.

69. Stop Banging

Once when I was driving on Highway 101 from Monterey to San Francisco I saw a huge sign on a warehouse by the side of the road. It made me pull over and just stare in amazement.

DO NOT KEEP BANGING ON DOOR.

STOP AND WAIT UNTIL DOOR OPENS.

What more could you need?

> *Change me Beloved into One who can wait*
> *in patience and faith until the right actions*
> *are shown. Grant me the ability to align*
> *with Your Will and honor Divine timing.*

70. But I Want *God* to *Ravish* Me!

Several times a week I get letters that say, "I love your writing but I don't *want* to be changed by the Divine. I'm great as I am." Or, "You know, Tosha, you should use different language and say, 'God, please help me . . .'"

Well, you have to understand. I'm not looking for a tame, safe route here. I *love* offering myself 100 percent to the Divine to be changed, overcome, ravaged, taken, kissed, or shifted in any way She/He/It desires!

I seriously wish the Great Self to take over.

Since I trust this Force of Love, only deeper authenticity and peace can come if It's invited completely. You're not going to mutate into something you hate. You're beckoning your own wise, compassionate soul to lead.

No need to offer 30 percent to the Divine like a holiday sale at Kohl's and keep the rest for the ego.

When *all* is offered to the Divine, you're carried by Providence into your own true Self. What's in the way, falls away. This is available to anyone passionate enough to ask. Yes, the mind gets scared to "lose control," but it never actually had any in the first place.

This invitation is not about passivity. The right actions *do* get shown at the right time, sometimes vigorously. It just takes practice if you're someone who, in a tizzy of fear, has tried micromanaging the whole galaxy.

Actually, the Sufi poets like Hafiz and Rumi had their own versions of this prayer: "TAKE me, Lord, do what You will. I am totally Yours!"

So I've got no need to hold back and make the words safer, nicer, or softer. Even Hafiz wrote, "Stop your teacup talk of Love."

Just take me, take me, take me.

Luckily you don't have to have lived six hundred years ago in Persia to do this.

This place, this time, wherever you are, works quite well.

Ravishing is eternally available.

Change me Divine Beloved into One who welcomes Your intercession. Release my fear of surrender. Help me trust that by yielding to You, my deepest, wisest, Highest Self, all will be well.

Epilogue: The Tiniest Cup

I have a favorite Vietnamese restaurant in the East Bay I love to visit. I'll never forget the first time I went there.

When the waiter asked me if I wanted tea, I said yes. But I was shocked when he brought a huge pot, and a tiny cup, barely bigger than a thimble. "Do you think I could have a larger cup?" I asked. "Otherwise I'll be here forever."

He smiled radiantly. "Well, actually *that* is the purpose. In my culture, it's meant to take a long time. And you're meant to slow down and enjoy every small sip in each moment. Then you notice and savor every drop. We think it's odd in your country that most people want more and more all the time . . . and in a hurry at that.

"Slow down, allow it to take as long as it wants to take. The tea will show you."

He said it with so much love, I agreed.

> *Change me Divine Beloved into One who can completely enjoy the moment as it is. May I release all hurry, relaxing and accepting the present moment. Let me be fully and happily in the Now.*

171

Tosha Answers Your Questions

✦ Sometimes I have trouble with these prayers spiritually since to me they imply that God is separate from us.

I totally see how you might think this. At first, it might sound like "Oh, we're suffering and we're asking God like some guy in the sky to shift us." But this can be viewed through a different lens, like how the Sufi poets, like Rumi or Hafiz, saw God. To them, the Divine was the Beloved, both inside and outside oneself. And even the illusion of separation was part of the great love affair with this Force.

So to me, God is everything, inside, outside, ALL of it. Yet we often get hung up with a certain problem by relying on the ego to try to solve it. When we invoke the Divine to "shift" us, we invite the Highest part of OURSELVES to take over. So, to me, there's no separation at all, but it takes a spirit of experimentation. I recommend just trying it with a sticky problem and see what happens.

✦ How can you use these prayers to handle upsetting emotions?

These prayers are wonderful for difficult emotions like pain, fear, jealousy, resentment, really anything. Their purpose is not to block or erase the emotions but to deeply feel them and then let them go, without blaming ourselves for having them in the first place! I mean, emotions of all kinds just come with being in a human body, right?

So I often use CMPs like, *"Change me Divine into One who can feel this fully and then release it."* Or, *"Change me Divine into One who can accept myself completely as I go through this and then let it go, offering all to Your grace."* It's amazing how they create the room to accept the emotion, honor it, and then move on at the right time.

✦ I feel so guilty when I recite these prayers. Aren't I delegating my small self-responsibilities to God when I say some of these?

I found this question interesting. To me, the purpose of the small self IS to take direction from the Inner Divine! So I think the deepest "responsibility" of the small self is to invite the Divine to show the way.

So, let's say you're scared you might not make your rent payment. These prayers aren't saying don't pay your rent. Rather you can say a CMP like, *"Change me Divine Beloved into One who always trusts every need is met. Let me always move in the flow of Your Abundance."* And that might bring a whole series of events; you follow signs as they come. The prayers raise your vibration, open doors, and literally shift you from the inside. They're definitely not an indication of passivity or irresponsibility as you follow the leads. The right actions get shown.

✦ How do you use CMP? Do you say them out loud, silently, memorize them, what?

It really doesn't matter. People who are familiar with my writing usually realize quickly that I'm not big on "rules," as your own heart and inner Self will often show you the best way to use them. Each person is different. I think many systems and programs are filled with endless rules because people aren't taught to trust what feels right inside.

✦ How long do they take to work? How often do you say them?

These are rather magical in that they seem to operate differently all the time, depending on the person, topic, willingness, openness, all kinds of things. You can say them as often as you like. Certainly they are good to say the moment you realize you've fallen into old, negative habits and patterns.

But it's not like the South Beach Diet: Eat these things and you'll lose ten pounds in a week. Some prayers literally work instantly because the person is so very ready. Others, where say there is more resistance, may take weeks or even months.

Sometimes you think a prayer isn't "working" but in fact the shift is growing hidden or underground like the roots of a tree. And then suddenly you wake up one day feeling absolutely transformed! You don't know when it happened, but it was growing inside all along.

✦ **I'd like to do CMP to get my partner to clean the house. Will this work?**

Hey, thank you for making me giggle. No, because they are only for you. But here's what will often work. You can do a CMP like, *"Change me into One who fully offers this home and partnership to You. If it's meant to be, let our home belong to You and let everything be cleaned and handled in the perfect way. Make me be open to a miracle. Release me from all past grievances and resentment."*

I have a friend who used this prayer, and years of anger toward her mate fell away. Funny enough, suddenly her mate started cleaning!

✦ **Are these a substitute for therapy or other healing methods?**

Well, these don't replace such things. However, they often work mysteriously when other forms do not. I think it's because some forms of therapy, coaching, and counseling only work on "improving the small self." They help people feel better about themselves in the moment without actually inviting a larger Wisdom to take over.

We've all experienced this. Someone goes through years of therapy and becomes very articulate about her problem, yet it remains. Once it is offered entirely to Divine Intervention, the miraculous can finally enter. Perhaps you'll be guided to a new therapist or modality. Or perhaps the problem will just vanish. I've seen this many times.

This works because it finally makes the Divine the Source of all healing. In many systems, people view a particular healer or teacher as the Source. This is different. It says the Wisdom is within You; God is invited to take the lead and create whatever changes are needed.

✦ **I feel so passive doing this. I'm an Aries type of action person, so am I supposed to say these and just sit there?**

A big misconception is that these prayers mean passivity. In fact, they're based in offering the problem to the Divine and taking action as you are shown. Believe me, if you have sincerely offered the issue over, God will show the actions that are needed. They arise spontaneously and organically once the prayer is said. Sometimes immediately, sometimes later.

However, often the guidance is to wait. Sometimes once the prayers are said, there's nothing to do but wait until the Divine lines things up.

I promise you, once you've really given the prayer over with sincerity, the Divine will inspire the right action at the right time. So it's not passivity at all, although sometimes you need patience. (Oh, and there's a Change Me Prayer for that!)

Actually these prayers are similar to the kind of advice that comes through a system like the *I Ching*. You act when it's time to act, you wait when it's not. Your own heart shows you.

✦ **If everything is perfect as it is, why ask to be changed?**

Here's the simplest answer I can give to this. These prayers are not challenging the innate perfection of the Universe as it is. They address your own lack of harmony with What Is. They allow *you* to move into harmony, and they show the actions to let the Divine lead the way.

✦ **How are CMP any different from saying, "Help me do this."**

The issue is really the agenda behind the "help me" prayer. Let's say you secretly covet your neighbor's property. It's driving you crazy because you WANT to own it. A small-self agenda would say, "Dear God, help me get that land. I want it. I'll visualize myself living there until I get it."

But a Change Me Prayer could say, *"Let me trust that I'll always have what's right for me. May I always know my own abundance and protection by You."* They're always geared to a Divine agenda.

So many prayers from the small self really don't address the true issue anyway. For example, at the bottom of that prayer for the neighbor's land is simply fear and scarcity. So asking to trust that the right place is available lets you have faith that you'll always have what you need.

Your own sense of inner abundance develops. And that's what matters, not getting what belongs to someone else.

✦ Can I use CMP to help manifest what I want?

This question made me smile. There are a thousand books out there about how to try to manifest what the small self wants. This is actually quite different. CMPs invite a DIVINE agenda, rather than a shopping list from the small self. So these actually invite a Divine plan to lead your life.

But here's the beautiful irony. As you do them over time, raging desires become preferences. Soon, you start realizing miracles, small and large, are sprouting everywhere you go. Soon, you stop thinking, "How can I manifest this or that?" You start realizing many secret longings of your heart are actually arriving on their own!

Eventually you spontaneously think during any problem, "How can I let the Divine take this over? How can I let God use me for the Highest?"

Life becomes transformed, freed from the burden of "trying to manifest" this or that.

A whole new life begins.

Change Me Prayers Quick Guide

Here's the single prayer I use more often than any other, for it can reliably take almost anyone into a high state of awareness, releasing all fear and grasping. Try it and see. The rest of this guide consists of Change Me Prayers on a variety of topics. I hope by reading them you'll begin to feel comfortable making up your own as well!

Divine Beloved, change me into One who can give with complete ease and abundance, knowing You are the unlimited Source of All.

Let me be an easy open conduit for Your prosperity.

Let me trust that my own needs are always met in amazing ways and it's safe to give freely as my heart guides.

And equally, please change me into One who can feel wildly open to receiving.

Let me know my own value, beauty, and worthiness without question.

Let me allow others the supreme pleasure of giving to me.

Let me feel worthy to receive in every possible way.

And protect me, dear Lord, from those whose hearts may be closed. Let me extend kindness to all who need, feeling compassion and understanding in even the hardest situations.

Change me into One who can fully love, forgive, and accept myself, so I may carry your Light without restriction.

Let everything that needs to go, go.

Let everything that needs to come, come.

I am utterly Your own.

I am You.

You are Me.

We are One.

All is well.

In seemingly hopeless situations, never forget that God can make a way from No Way.

And the deeper your detachment, the greater the openness to miracles.

Change me Divine Beloved into One who can be open to Your will in all situations, even ones that are baffling in the moment. Guide my way, let me trust that all doors open at the right time, even those that are hidden.

Let me only wish for Your Divine plan in all its forms. Melt me, let me surrender and trust.

I am Yours.

You are Mine.

We are One.

All is well.

ACCEPTANCE

Change me Divine Beloved into one who willingly embraces what You send (the easy and the hard) as if it had come from My own heart. And let me trust that even the most unfathomable mysteries will be revealed over time. Change me into One who can trust what's unfolding.

I am Yours.

You are Mine.

We are One.

All is well.

AUTHENTICITY

Change me Divine Beloved into One who can fully embrace my authentic self. Release me from the prison of pleasing and adapting to the expectations of others. Free me from the fear of judgment. Let me step into my own glorious true Self exactly as You made me. Allow me to know that I am enough, exactly as I am.

AWAKENING TO INNER DIVINITY

Divine Beloved, may I only wish Your wishes for me. Let me see myself as you see me. May I know my own Divinity in every moment and may our desires be One.

Grant me peace, happiness, and contentment, trusting that whatever is meant to happen, will always happen. May I be a vehicle for all You wish to occur.

Change me Divine Beloved into One who can easily offer you even the deepest desires, knowing You already have the perfect plan for me. You know the longings of my own heart.

May I sense when to wait, and when to act, and always follow Your lead.

May I always let what wants to go, go and what wants to come, come.

I am Yours.

You are Mine.

We are One.

All is well.

BIRTHDAY

Divine Beloved, change me into One who joyously embraces Your Plan for me. Every day let me be born anew. Fill me with Your courage and enthusiasm, free from all fears and resistances, wishing only to serve You in every way. Grant me patience and faith as I take the steps You show.

Release me from old doubts, fears and confusion, knowing every step will be revealed at the right time.

May I trust all doors will fling open in Divine time.

Use me according to Your will.

BODY

Change me Divine Beloved into One who sees the beauty and miraculousness of my own body however it is.

Change me into One who always knows my own value and worth in every situation. Teach me how to love myself as You love me. May I shower myself with the love, patience, and acceptance that my own heart longs for and deserves. May I be deeply kind to myself.

CHANGE ME

Change me into One who can actually LET go and let You change me.

Allow me to breathe, relax, and easily invite You to guide my way.

Change me Beloved into One who so trusts my connection and confidence in You that I can invite You into ANY aspect of my life.

May I trust that You show me all the right actions at every moment. Let me know we are One and I am safe.

CLARITY

Change me Divine Beloved into One who can clearly recognize Your signs and plans for me. When Your Will is veiled, please make it clear and show me the way!

COMPASSION

Change me Divine Beloved into One who always knows and honors my own inner worth. Let me take nothing personally when the actions of others feel hurtful. May I feel open-hearted compassion for those who are suffering.

I am Yours. You are Mine. We are One.

CONSCIOUS LIVING

Change me Divine Beloved into One who trusts that the highest is always happening and all unfolds in the best way. May I be a vehicle for the miraculous and live purely with positive intent.

DELAYS

Change me Divine Beloved into One who knows and trusts that every delay happens for my benefit. May I relax and ride the Flow of life with faith that all true needs will always be handled. Let me always trust I am guided to the right actions at the right time.

I am Yours.

You are mine.

We are One.

All is well.

DESIRE

Change me Divine Beloved into One who can easily offer you even the deepest desires, knowing in every cell that You already have the perfect plan for me. You completely know my heart.

Allow me to let go and trust you in every way by waiting or taking action as guided, and always, always following Your lead.

Help me let what wants to go, go and what wants to come, come.

Divine Beloved, change me into One whose every desire TRULY belong to You. Grant me detachment, patience, and calm.

Let me fully trust Your plan.

If this idea is Yours, let it bloom the perfect way.

And if it is not, FREE me from its grip completely.

I long for Your desires alone.

Divine Beloved, change me into One who can offer my heart's desires to Your loving hands. May I trust Your complete guidance in every moment.

Change me into One who can offer You even my deepest longings. Let them now be Yours to do with as You will. Make me Your very own.

If this current idea is Your own, then please, lead the

way, filling me with patience and faith. And if this idea is NOT Your will, then free me from attachment so all may unfold as You desire, trusting there is a perfect plan.

I am Yours.

You are Mine.

We are One.

All is well.

DISAPPOINTMENT

Discontent and disappointment in the present reliably draw the same in the future.

Change me Divine Beloved into One who is able to embrace the present as it is with gratitude, or at least detached amusement. May I trust that even what seems like a disappointment may simply pave the way for a perfect Divine plan at the right time.

I am Yours.

You are Mine.

We are One.

All is well.

DIVINE FAITH

Divine Beloved, change me into One who lets You protect and guide me in every moment. Fill me with Faith, even in the most trying of circumstances.

May I always know Your radiant protection is present in every moment.

DIVINE GUIDANCE

Divine Beloved, may I feel safe and guided by Your Love. Take over my body and mind, show me the way. Guide me always to the right actions at the right time. May I always feel immersed in Your Love, protected from fear and negativity.

Divine Beloved, let me only wish what You wish for me. May I see myself as You see me. Let me know my own Divinity in every moment. May I know I am You, and may our desires be One.

May the Highest that is meant to happen, happen in me and through me.

May I be a vehicle for all You wish to occur.

Change me into One who can breathe, relax, and rest in Your arms.

DIVINE PROSPERITY

May I always trust the Divine Flow.

May I always know there is Enough.

Change me into One who always trusts You.

Change me into One who feels worthy to open up to true Abundance.

DIVINE RELATIONSHIPS

My Beloved, free me from attachment to ANY situations that do not serve my highest good and Your Divine Will. Whoever needs to come, let them come. Whoever needs to go, let them go. My needs are always met.

I am Yours.

You are mine

We are One.

DIVINE SURRENDER

Take me over and do what You will.
　　I am Yours alone.
　　Just take me over and do what You will.
　　Make me Yours.
　　You are Mine.
　　We are One.
　　All is well.

DIVINE TIMING

Change me my Beloved into One who can breathe and relax completely into your perfect Divine timing. Let me trust that everything unfolds exactly on schedule for the highest good. May I trust that every seeming delay is a great unseen blessing. Every day it becomes easier to breathe, relax, and receive in faith and trust.

Divine Beloved, change me into One who can trust Your timing and wait according to Your will, knowing that everything happens as needed for my own highest evolution and through Your Love.

And thank You for protecting me from what I'm not yet ready to receive and for giving me the faith that all occurs on Your Divine schedule.

I stand in the center of my reality as a spark of the Divine. Let all that wishes to come, come. Let all that wishes to go, go. My life unfolds in Divine perfection.

DIVINE TRUST

Change me Divine Beloved into One who trusts where You guide me.

May I always have the faith to follow Your lead.

Let me bless life's unfolding in all ways that are right for me.

May I always trust You.

May I always know We are One.

DIVINE WORTH

Divine Beloved, change me into One who every day remembers who I REALLY am—a living, breathing conduit for Love.

May I wake up to who I actually AM:
All I encounter.
May I be carried by Divine Grace in every moment.
May I know my true nature as Love itself.

EASE

O Beloved, change me into One who knows how to relax completely, sleep deeply, and receive all the blessings of every moment as they arise.

Change me into One who deeply trusts the Divine plan. May I feel gratitude and ease every day.

May I remain centered in all conditions, even those which are volatile or difficult. Hold me in my center O Lord. I relax in calm peace, knowing all is in perfect Divine Order.

Change me into One who trusts Your process and knows I am being guided to the perfect resolution of all seeming dilemmas. The Divinely right solutions are already selected and being born. I can breathe, relax, receive, and be guided.

I am safe. All is well.

EGO

Take me over and do what You will.
    I am Yours alone.
    Fill the space between us.
    Make me Yours.

EMERGENCIES

This issue now belongs completely to You, my Divine Beloved. The perfect solution *already* is selected and I will be guided to it in the perfect way and time. Please open me to Your miraculous will! Release any doubt and allow me to gratefully receive Your solution. I am Yours.

FEAR

Divine Beloved, please free me from the noose of my fears! May I be used by You in service to the Light.

Divine Beloved, please change me into One who feels completely safe and guided by Your Love. *Take over* my body and mind, show me the way in every moment. Guide me to the right actions at the right time.

And let me hold a light so *strong* I am protected from any fear or negativity in others. May I be a vessel for the Light for all who need.

FEELINGS

Change me O Divine Beloved into One who can have my feelings without fear or judgment. Let me accept them as holy expressions of my own inner Self. May I trust and accept myself fully.

May I honor and release all emotions, knowing my true Self is beyond duality. I offer You all my feelings to be blessed.

May I rest in Your arms as old wounds release and heal.

I am Yours, You are Mine, We are One.

All is well.

FLOW

I am always in the right place at the right time, moving with the Flow. Every day it becomes easier to stay *completely* in the moment. The Divine guides my every action and protects me in every way. Every transit brings the perfect blessings.

All is well.

Divine Beloved, change me into One who can move or not move in right timing. I am filled with the peace of God.

Divine Beloved, change me into One who can roll calmly and peacefully with the unfolding flow, holding my center amidst volatile shifts. All is well.

Change me Divine Beloved into One who moves with deep ease and allowing. Let me trust where the Flow is guiding me, knowing ALL unfolds in the right time and way.

I am Yours, You are Mine. We are One. All is well.

FOR EVERY OVERWHELMING DILEMMA, ALL-PURPOSE CHANGE ME PRAYER

CHANGE ME DIVINE BELOVED INTO ONE WHO KNOWS HOW THE HECK TO DO THIS!

Take me over, lead the way. I offer *all* into Your competent hands so that You guide my *every* action.

FORGIVENESS

Change me Divine Beloved into One who knows without question that You are the unlimited Source of all. May I forgive anyone who has hurt me, knowing that You alone provide for all my needs in the most surprising and abundant ways.

May I release remaining blame or anger toward others. May I be freed from the noose of resentment, jealousy, and victimization. May I forgive any perceived injustice, trusting that whatever needs to happen will ultimately happen in the right time and way.

All of my needs are always abundantly met. There is enough for everyone. And may Destiny use me in the highest way for the good of All.

FRIENDS / COMMUNITY

Change me O Beloved into One who trusts that the perfect needed connections always arrive at the right time and way. For You are the One arriving in disguise as each person, place, or thing. Let me trust the way You open every door as needed.

GIVING

Change me into One who can give abundantly, knowing I live in a constant state of grace and prosperity.

Change me Divine Beloved into One who is wildly comfortable receiving.

HELP

Change me Divine Beloved into One who always allows the right assistance to arrive. I welcome Your help in every way and take absolute delight in receiving it.

INNER CHILD

Change me into One who can easily soothe, love, and care for the Inner Child who may grow fearful or impatient. Let me easily send that Love to take care of It in every way.

Every day I grow more and more filled with Divine courage, patience, ease, and calm.

All is well.

INTUITION

Please, my Divine Beloved, change me into One who can always heed my deepest instincts. Let me experience the pleasure of trusting my intuition at all times. May I move with ever-deeper confidence and faith.

Divine Beloved, please change me into One who can embody all my heart knows. May I live in harmony with my inner knowing.

Divine Beloved, change me into One who can trust and hear my own inner guidance. May I relax, breathe, receive, and enjoy the ride! Let me hold the Light for all who need.

Please help me trust my intuition, honor my own inner power, and let my instincts guide at all times.

May I never forget the true power is Yours alone.

INVITING THE DIVINE

Divine Beloved, change me into One who remembers to invite You into every aspect of my Being, allowing perfect solutions to arise in the right time and way. Let me trust You and our Oneness more every day.

Change me, O Beloved, into One who feels so trusting of my connection and confidence in You that I can invite You with an open heart into ANY aspect of my life.

Change me into One who can easily make prayers of invitation and love from my own heart's longing. Let me trust my own voice. Let me trust that You show me all the right actions at every moment. Let me know we are One and I am safe.

LOSS

Divine Beloved, change me into One who trusts You are the Ultimate Source for all. Let me know abundance of every kind comes from You alone. May I neither fear loss nor cling to gain, knowing You take care of me in EVERY possible way. Let me trust that any seeming loss can be replenished according to Your will in the most perfect, synchronous, and beautiful ways. May I relax and enjoy Your gifts to me.

LOST

Change me Divine Beloved into One who trusts Your plan fully, and with total faith—even when transitory appearances make it look like You don't know what You're doing! May I always trust Your guidance. Grant me patience, faith, and clarity. Just show me the next step.

All is well.

MYSTERY

Change me Divine Beloved into One who offers all current mysteries with great ease and joy to You alone. Show me Your plan, in even the most baffling situations. Take my fears and worries. You alone guide my heart. Let me always trust that all actions are shown at the appointed time, and all doors open as needed.

Change me Divine Beloved into One who can comfortably rest in the mystery. May I trust my life will bloom in perfect ways.

NEW CYCLE

Change me Divine Beloved into One who knows that the perfect unfolding is always occurring, even in times of invisible transition. Let me trust that all unseen growth will be known at the right time. Let me have faith in Your plan.

May I welcome this new cycle as it slowly births.

Let me bless its unfolding.

May I feel worthy to receive the highest and know my own value.

May I be an uplifting force for the good of All.

OBSTACLES

Change me Divine Beloved into One who willingly embraces Your obstacles and tests knowing they come from Your love. May I trust Your plan, knowing it carries me to ever-deeper awareness and wholeness. I am Your own.

Change me Divine Beloved into One who can bless and welcome what currently Is. And thank You for KEEPING me from what I do not yet need. I bow to every "seeming" obstacle, knowing it can dissolve in an instant when the time is ripe.

May I trust Your plan in every way, knowing the right steps get shown at the right time, and I will always know them.

OPPORTUNITIES

The perfect opportunities are ALREADY selected to allow my life to unfold exactly as needed according to Divine Love. I can relax, breathe, and allow things to reveal themselves in the right time. I will always know the perfect actions to take as the leads are shown.

PATIENCE

My Beloved, please change me into One who can trust Your timing. May I peacefully wait according to Your will, knowing that everything happens for my highest evolution.

Thank you for protecting me from what I am not yet ready to receive. May I trust that all occurs perfectly on Your Divine schedule.

PROBLEMS

Change me Divine Beloved into One who invites You into every aspect of my Being, allowing perfect solutions to arise in the right time and way. Let me trust our Oneness more each day.

All difficult situations are now in Your hands. I can relax and let my intuition lead the way, trusting that the answers are already being born.

Inner Beloved, thank You for changing me into One who patiently embraces even the most baffling problems. Let me daily relax and invite Your help. May I be guided with ease.

Change me into One who trusts the right solutions to every need or problem are already selected.

I am carried and guided by Divine grace in every moment.

May I always know my true nature is Love itself.

RECEIVING

Please change me Divine Beloved into One who can feel wildly open to receiving.

Let me know my own value, beauty, and worthiness without question.

Let me allow others the supreme pleasure of giving to me.

Let me feel worthy to receive in every possible way.

Change me into One who can fully love, forgive, and accept myself, so I may carry Your Light without restriction.

Let everything that needs to go, go.

Let everything that needs to come, come.

I am utterly Your own.

You are Me.

I am You.

We are One.

All is well.

RELAX

O Beloved, change me into One who knows how to relax completely, sleep deeply, and receive all the blessings of every moment exactly as it presents itself with ease and gratitude.

RELEASING

Let me release all that is outgrown and align with the Divine for the highest unfolding. The perfect routes are already selected and will unfold naturally and easily.

Let me know my true nature as Love.

Divine Beloved, change me into One who easily releases all that wishes to go. Let me move with courage and ease. As I stand on the threshold of the new, let me trust that all that needs to happen *will* happen in the most uplifting and joyous ways. What is needed is *already* known. I will be guided, shown, and provided for in every way.

All is well.

RESENTMENT

Change me Divine Beloved into One who easily releases all resentments or wounds, knowing You alone constantly refill my cup with abundance and peace. In my union with You, I endlessly receive all I need.

I am Yours. You are Mine. All is well.

SELF-WORTH

Change me into One who truly knows her own self-worth.

Allow me to say what I want and need in a relationship, without the fear of rejection or abandonment. Free me from those who are incapable of giving. Allow me to always feel fully deserving to receive.

Change me Divine Beloved into One who KNOWS without doubt my own worthiness. Let me always know I never need convince ANYONE of my value.

Change me Divine Beloved into One who can absolutely inundate myself with love, acceptance, and compassion.

Let me do so and then may I pour this love with abandon into the world.

Change me O Divine Beloved into One who always knows my own value and worth in EVERY situation. Teach me how to love myself as You love Me. May I shower myself with love, patience, and acceptance. Let me be deeply kind, inside and out.

Change me Divine Beloved into One who can fully love and accept myself every day. Let me see my own beauty and worthiness. Guide my way, let me be a vehicle for Your Love. Guide my actions; take me where you wish me to go. Transform me as You will.

SOUL MATE

Change me Divine Beloved into One who can trust that the perfect person has already been selected. In the right place and time we shall meet, for You know every true desire of my heart. May I only desire what You desire for me.

STAGNATION

Divine Beloved, change me into One who happily releases ALL that is stagnant and outlived. Whether those are physical objects, clutter, old beliefs, destructive habits, or useless emotions, transform me into One who easily releases what I no longer need.

May I be a clear vessel for Love to serve the highest good. May I release all that wishes to go, to make room for the New that is headed my way.

SUPPORT

Change me Divine Beloved into One who always allows the right assistance to arrive. I welcome your help in every way and take absolute delight in receiving it.

I am Yours.
You are Mine.
We are One.
All is well.

SURRENDER

Change me Divine Beloved into One who fully trusts Your path for me. Whatever You wish, I am Yours. If these desires are Your own, then please show the way, open the road at the right time. And if you DON'T wish them, then please, please free me from this prison of longing. Grant me patience and ease.

Change me into One who longs to surrender to you. May any perceived problems fill Your beautiful arms. The solutions are already picked. You know every longing and fear in my heart. You show the way even in the dark.

I am Yours.

You are Mine.

We are One.

All is well.

TRUTH

Change me Divine Beloved into One who can stand in Her Truth in all circumstances. Let me know the pleasure of honoring the inner voice and feelings no matter what.

Take me over and give me the right words and actions at all times.

I am Yours.

UNIQUENESS

Change me Divine Beloved into One who loves and adores all the quirks, flaws, and wounds of this incarnate being. Let me rest in Your arms and accept myself wildly, completely and precisely as I am, perfect in my glorious imperfection.

And may I love others that way too.

VALENTINE

Change me Divine Beloved into One who can be a most wonderful and true companion to myself. Change me into One who is patient, kind, and accepting of myself in every way. May I easily love, accept, and honor my own beautiful Self, knowing my own worthiness and value.

I am Yours.

You are Mine.

We are One.

WAITING

Change me Divine Beloved into One who can wait patiently, respecting the timing of the Universe. May I rest and refill with full gratitude as You line up the next chapter.

May I relax in Your arms until the proper actions get shown.

I am Yours.

You are mine.

We are One.

All is well.

Change me into One who knows how to let go, trust, and wait on the Will of Heaven. May I trust that the Universe guides my steps in the most surprising and abundant ways at the right time IF I invite it.

Change me Divine Beloved into One who always knows that the perfect unfolding is ALWAYS occurring, even in times of invisible transitions. May I trust all unseen growth will open any needed doors in the right ways, at the right time. Let me always trust Your plan.

Every day I grow more and more filled with Divine courage, patience, ease, and calm.

WILDLY OPEN

Change me Divine Beloved into One who is wildly open to *whatever* needs to occur at this turning point. Let me trust where You guide my own heart. Let me know that perfect actions are shown at the right time. Fill me with patience and clarity. And let me be genuinely kind to myself and others.

All is well.

Change me O Beloved into One who is WILDLY open and trusting of Your plan despite any current uncertainty. Let me trust that You know *exactly* where the heck You are guiding me, even if this is not currently apparent.

WORRY

Change me Divine Beloved into One who is freed from the noose of fear and worry. Let me trust that if You want me to do something, You'll either give me the ability or send the right help.

WOUNDS

Change me Divine Beloved into One who can inundate myself with love, compassion, and acceptance every day—even the hidden parts, even the wounds. May I feel whole and complete knowing we are One.

I am Yours.
You are Mine.
We are One.
All is well.

WRITE YOUR OWN PRAYERS

ACKNOWLEDGMENTS

This book would never have come together without the inspiration, kindness, and hand-holding of numerous people. I feel the Divine used each one to help me bring it to you.

My dearest friend Alice Turkel was my steady editor and muse from her little home on the prairie in upstate New York. Her acerbic wit, compassionate heart, literary insight, and funny songs in a fake Yiddish accent all kept me going during hard times. She and her husband, Gray, are my spiritual family.

Matt Klein, my manager and friend, arrived exactly when I needed him most and has offered daily support, kindness, and inspiration of every kind. I am deeply grateful.

Dr. Lissa Rankin has been a generous advocate and friend from the beginning. She inspires me with her open heart, playful energy, and ability to be more effortlessly prolific than almost anyone I've ever met. I thank her for the beautiful Foreword.

Johanna Castillo has been a most wonderful and insightful editor at Atria. She's able to see things when I'm not, like dreaming up the magnificent structure of this book. I feel blessed to have been led to her, and I adore her. (And actually, the entire staff at Atria are fantastic. Thank you Divine for finally guiding me to the right publishing house!)

247

Melanie Bates was also a kind and astonishingly efficient editor and organizer for this project. Thank heavens I was led to her.

Dr. Christiane Northrup has been a consistent goddess pal and soul-mirror. Her help has been invaluable, and I love our frequent hilarious, raucous phone calls.

Stephanie Tade, my agent and friend, has been invaluable. I am so grateful for her warm, loving, humorous yet no-nonsense approach. She truly couldn't be a better fit.

Gail Gonzales whisked in out of nowhere to make a video of this work and has become a wonderfully entertaining friend and advocate. Thank you Gail!

Also I am daily grateful for the inspired writings and teachings of Adyashanti, Nisargadata Maharaj, Rumi, and Hafiz.

Also thank you, thank you, thank you to David Lein, Seraphina Atemasov, Heather Mahan, Lisa Ravaioli and Kristina Militante, Melanie Fife, Krista Koehs, Sarah Buscho, Sarah Drew, Kerry Haworth, and my brothers Michael and Scott Silver. Many others, too, so please forgive me if I forgot anyone.

Finally THANK YOU to the twenty thousand gorgeous, eloquent, inspired old souls on my Facebook author page. Your questions, comments, love, and reverent irreverence often inspired my writing. I feel blessed to be connected to you.

LET THE DIVINE LEAD THE WAY

"This book will change your life. I refer to it regularly."

—Christiane Northrup, M.D., *New York Times* bestselling author

Put down the heavy load of fervent hopes and fears about how things are supposed to be and delight in the spectacular show that is our life.

PROUDLY PUBLISHED BY ATRIA BOOKS

Pick up or download your copy today!